MW00511290

Praise for

HOW TO SUCCEED IN THE RELATIONSHIP ECONOMY

'A better relationship with your customer starts with truly understanding your customer. While designers often think they intuitively understand their customers, using both quantitative and qualitative data analysis described in this book can truly give new insights, which lead to better decision making.'

—JELLE PRINS, design manager, Uber

'This book takes the B.S. out of so much blather about reader revenue. As the authors point out—with great case histories— subscriptions start with great content and prosper with smarts that only ongoing intelligence gleaned from data can sustain. This is a great primer for all who believe in the growing power of reader revenue for news companies.'

—KEN DOCTOR, president, Newsonomics

'Mather and NRC look into the future of subscription economics as few can. How to Succeed in the Relationship Economy *elegantly captures the change in the consumer landscape we are witnessing. Companies using data-driven subscription models are making Darwinian leaps over their predecessors. This book is a must-read for anyone serious about evolving their business.'*

—STACY SPIKES, cofounder, MoviePass

'In our data-intelligence infancy, we need forward-thinking and experienced practitioners. The authors of How to Succeed in the Relationship Economy *are among them, and their book is a real milestone in a journey every business should have embarked upon a while ago. It's never too late to learn from the best, and I encourage you to dive deep into this most up-to-date guide available on data and customer experience.'*

—VINCENT PEYREGNE, CEO, WAN-IFRA

'As businesses, especially in the publishing industry, move increasingly toward subscription models, they may feel that they can no longer have meaningful relationships with their customers. The authors of How to Succeed in the Relationship Economy *have outlined in great detail the ways in which thoughtful use of data analytics can allow for a new kind of customer relationship, one informed by real information about what users want and how they relate to your products. The authors provide a fascinating, real-world guide for businesses who want to harness the power of smart analytics to create meaningful and sustainable customer relationships.'*

—DAVID CLINCH, global news editor, Storyful

'Relationships are the new fuel of our economy. They drive our personal and private behaviours and choices, but they also define our engagement with companies and brands. We have moved from a transactional, object-based economy to a relational, subject-based economy. It's no longer product benefits that drive our choices but goodwill grounded in relationships. How to Succeed in the Relationship Economy *is a timely book, not only because it helps us understand this shift but also because it provides us with the essential tools to manage it. By synthesising the empathy and creativity of customer experience with the precision and rigor of data analytics, this book helps us build sustainable value through relationships, which will bring us one step closer to a truly human-centred economy.'*

—ERIK ROSCAM ABBING, director, Livework Netherlands

'Matt Lindsay pioneered the segmented pricing of newspaper subscribers that allowed newspapers all over America to yield-manage their print-subscription revenue and drive substantial new profitable revenue to their income statements. He did this at a time when newspapers desperately needed incremental sources of revenue. I can think of very few people who have singlehandedly done more to help the financial plight of newspapers than the author of this book.'

—JIM MORONEY, publisher and CEO, The Dallas Morning News

'I am impressed by the authors' capability to bring sophisticated and holistic data-analytics expertise down to real business and value creation. The use case presented in the book is an easy-to-understand proof for successfully implementing a data-driven strategy.'

—GEORG SAUER, vice president business intelligence finance, 1&1 Internet SE

'Many companies claim to put their customers first but fail in doing so. Whether it's the short-term sales objectives that prevail, the product-driven way of working that is difficult to change, or because it's just not that easy to prove the value of data and analytics to the business, many companies struggle in transitioning to a customer-driven organisation. Matt, Xavier, and Matthijs have done outstanding work in achieving customer-driven growth and are sharing their learnings and best practices in this hands-on guide into customer-led decision making for business growth. If you truly want to succeed in putting your customers first, read this book!'

—JIMMY DE VREEDE, business consultant, Yourzine

'How to Succeed in the Relationship Economy puts data to practice and is a concrete source of information on how to build an organisation that harnesses the power of data effectively.'

—SLAVEN MANDIC, CEO, WayneParkerKent

How to Succeed in the

RELATIONSHIP
ECONOMY

How to Succeed in the

RELATIONSHIP
ECONOMY

Make Data Work for You

Empathise with Customers

Grow Valuable Relationships

XAVIER VAN LEEUWE   MATT LINDSAY   MATTHIJS VAN DE PEPPEL

Published by Advantage, Charleston, South Carolina.
Member of Advantage Media Group.

ADVANTAGE is a registered trademark, and the Advantage colophon is a trademark of Advantage Media Group, Inc.

Printed in the United States of America.

10 9 8 7 6 5 4 3 2 1

ISBN: 978-1-59932-649-8
LCCN: 2017932801

Cover design by Katie Biondo.
Interior design by George Stevens.

This publication is designed to provide accurate and authoritative information in regard to the subject matter covered. It is sold with the understanding that the publisher is not engaged in rendering legal, accounting, or other professional services. If legal advice or other expert assistance is required, the services of a competent professional person should be sought.

Advantage Media Group is proud to be a part of the Tree Neutral® program. Tree Neutral offsets the number of trees consumed in the production and printing of this book by taking proactive steps such as planting trees in direct proportion to the number of trees used to print books. To learn more about Tree Neutral, please visit **www.treeneutral.com**.

Advantage Media Group is a publisher of business, self-improvement, and professional development books. We help entrepreneurs, business leaders, and professionals share their Stories, Passion, and Knowledge to help others Learn & Grow. Do you have a manuscript or book idea that you would like us to consider for publishing? Please visit **advantagefamily.com** or call **1.866.775.1696**.

To our most important relationships:
Annie, Arieke, and Wietske

TABLE OF CONTENTS

PREFACE

This book is the product of a fortuitous collaboration between NRC Media and Mather Economics. The organisations are complementary but very different. NRC Media is a Dutch publisher. Mather Economics is an American consulting firm. NRC has considerable expertise around customer relationships and customer experience, while Mather deals in big data and predictive analytics. We found that each side had much to offer the other, and we firmly believe that the product of our collaboration is worth sharing with a broad audience.

When the two companies met, NRC was facing challenges. Readership was declining, and advertisement income was decreasing. NRC had to pivot to prosper in the long term. Mather and NRC started working together and were able to turn decline into sustainable growth in both readership and revenue development. During the course of our multiyear effort to enhance the performance of NRC's subscription department through analytics and testing, team members from both companies realised they shared common perspectives on the importance of customer relationships and the power of data and analytics to enhance those relationships. In addition, the teams recognised that their combined efforts yielded a result greater than what each organisation could have achieved independently.

We hope you enjoy reading this book as much as we have enjoyed the learning journey that brought us to this point. Our goal is to help others, particularly those in dramatically changing industries such as the news media. We want you to succeed in your audience and revenue-growth goals. This book shares many case studies from hundreds of projects we have completed with companies in several industries, including several from our experience at NRC. We trust they are helpful in conveying the power of the concepts and tools presented here so you can grow personally and eventually go through profound change—building an organisation that is less gut driven, more data informed, empathetic to other people's needs, and with smoother financial returns for the long term. We wish you more fun in your work and to feel genuinely proud about establishing new and deeper relationships on this planet.

THIS BOOK IS FOR YOU

This book contains strategies for putting data to good use and making customers happy. Those strategies can be used by nearly any type of organisation. Both beginners and seasoned experts in the fields of data and customer experience will find new case studies and fresh insights that will help set out a strategy for long-term survival. There are practical case studies from banking, news media, telecommunications, and cable providers. We aim to stimulate the transformation of businesses and provide guidance in what to do next. Readers who will benefit most from this book include the following:

- *marketers, data analysts, and customer-experience specialists* who need inspiring and practical examples to reduce costs and increase revenue by using data and empathy

- *executives and board members* in the news industry and beyond who are interested in knowing how building relationships with their customers can build a healthier financial bottom line

- *entrepreneurs* who want to build a sustainable recurring-revenue model from scratch and who wish to understand where their customers will lead them

- *association leaders* who worry about declining membership support

- *academics and students* in the fields of business administration, analytics, economics, and customer experience

The Relationship Economy Is Here

After you woke up this morning, one of the first things you may have done was to check your mobile phone, powered by a monthly paid data plan. Then you may have taken a shower, used a razor from the Dollar Shave Club, and made coffee using ingredients from the organic-beans-of-the-month club. You possibly watched the morning news delivered via your cable-television service or read a daily delivered newspaper. You might have worked out at the gym where you are a member, or maybe used a monthly pass to take public transit to work. During the day you will use software in the cloud, like Microsoft Office 365. When you get home, you can watch Netflix or listen to music via Pandora or Spotify. At the end of the day, you close down the house and set your home security system.

Our days are packed with subscription services. The growth of subscription-based income has been widely observed and documented. The Subscription Economy Index has grown nine times faster than S&P 500 sales and four times faster than US retail sales over the past five years. Gartner, a leading information technology research and advisory company, predicts 80 per cent or more of software providers will offer their products as software-as-a-service by 2020.[1]

Why is the subscription model growing? Because we need a new sense of belonging. We are moving faster every day and spending less time in traditional communities like clubs, churches, civic organisations, and even family gatherings. We are becoming more individualised and speaking less to the people close to us.[2] As a result, people are connecting in other ways—through technology, in online communities, and through organisations and brands.[3]

While a growing number of businesses respond to this societal change by introducing a subscription model, the publishing business has known this model for ages. At NRC and Mather Economics, we have taken the subscription model a step further. We have started to harvest, cherish, and grow relationships because we found that to be the most profitable and rewarding thing to do with our customers. We see more businesses shifting their focus to

---

1   Zuora, "The Subscription Economy Index," 2016, https://www.zuora.com/resource/subscription-economy-index-2016/.

2   Robert Putnam, *Bowling Alone: The Collapse and Revival of American Community* (New York: Simon Shuster Paperbacks, 2001).

3   Robbie Baxter, *The Membership Economy* (McGraw-Hill Education, 2015).

developing relationships. That's why we feel we are evolving towards a Relationship Economy.[4]

In this economy, it's not enough to just build an outstanding product or have a laser focus on customer-centricity. It is also not only about analysing the right data. The Relationship Economy requires a change in company culture such that a focus on human relationships is augmented by analytics and led by front-line operators who know the customers.

This book will show how to use data and empathy to build relationships with customers. First of all, it describes a path to work with data whilst avoiding myths about big data. Contrary to the current trend of collecting more and more data, we propose to sometimes collect less data—or rather, to collect the *right* data that supports business goals.

Second, we marry two fields that have thus far lived and evolved independently. On the one hand there is the field of analytics, which is considered 'hard'. The importance of analytics is swiftly understood by board members. On the other hand there is customer experience, which has different methodologies, employs empathy, and is often described as a 'soft' field. Board members all too often do not realise that customer emotions are facts too.

We discovered that these two fields need each other to reach their full potential. Customer experience, when quantified, makes

---

4   Robbie Baxter (2015) states that we live in the titular 'Membership Economy'. However, at NRC we found not all of our relationships feel like 'memberships'. Some subscribers are just satisfied with the great journalism and services they receive; they don't identify themselves as 'members of the newspaper'. We believe the same applies to companies like Microsoft and Netflix. Their clients receive good products and services, but not all of them regard themselves as 'members of the Microsoft community' or 'members of the Netflix community'. Hence we prefer the term 'Relationship Economy'.

a 'soft' subject manageable and rigorous. Analytics comes to life when empathy towards customers is added. Relationships with customers will only grow when business processes are improved with insights from both data and from customers.

Using the insights and the tools described in this book can help organisations succeed in the evolving economy we live in.

AFTER READING THIS BOOK, YOU WILL BE ABLE TO

- build more relationships and grow your business;

- save customer stops;

- increase customer acquisition;

- optimise recurring revenue with data-informed yield management;

- create an effective data team;

- listen to customers through data;

- use Key Performance Indicators (KPIs) to change culture;

- explore the power of big data with common sense;

- use tools to turn data into actionable insights;

- understand the impact of pricing;

- find customers willing to build long-term relationships;

- invest in loyal customers without going bankrupt; and

- implement tools that discover deeper customer needs.

HOW TO READ THIS BOOK

This book is built around independent insights and case studies because we understand that time-pressed readers browse books according to their interests. The book is divided into five sections:

SECTION 1. MAKE DATA WORK FOR YOU (AND NOT AGAINST YOU)

Although big data is full of opportunities, it is also surrounded by hype. This first section shows you how to build analytical teams that unleash the power of KPIs whilst avoiding big-data pitfalls that cost time and money.

SECTION 2. BUILD VALUABLE RELATIONSHIPS

After building the data team and using the right data, it is time to understand the influence of pricing and employees on attracting and retaining customers who are willing to commit to a longer-term relationship.

SECTION 3. SUSTAIN RELATIONSHIPS BY IMPROVING CUSTOMER EXPERIENCE

This section explains how organisations get to a higher level and produce insights by stepping into their customers' shoes. Ideas are included to bridge organisational silos and get leadership support.

SECTION 4. ANALYTICAL TOOLS TO INCREASE THE VALUE OF RELATIONSHIPS

The concepts in the first three sections are supplemented in this section by six analytical tools that can be directly applied. They are presented in a practical business context, including case studies.

SECTION 5. CUSTOMER-EXPERIENCE TOOLS

In the same practical manner as the previous section, learn which instruments the field of customer experience uses to understand the needs of customers, develop better products, improve processes, and enrich data insights.

Feel free to jump back and forth in the book to find what interests you most. You can also read from start to finish, as the different ideas build on each other.

SECTION 1.

MAKE DATA WORK FOR YOU (AND NOT AGAINST YOU)

Big data is hot and full of opportunities. At the same time, there are a lot of pitfalls to avoid when applying data and business analytics. This section explains, step by step, how organisations make data work to meet their goals: by building no-nonsense analytical teams, unleashing the power of KPIs, and bringing common sense into big-data projects.

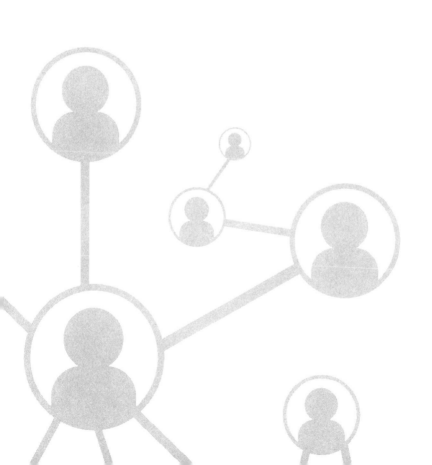

1. LET BUSINESS PEOPLE LEAD THE DATA TEAMS

A few years back, I entered the office for my first day on a new job. The very first question my new boss shot at me was, 'Do we keep the data warehouse?' It cost half a million euros per year just in maintenance, and there were millions of euros in sunk costs from the isolated staff of analysts who had worked at it for years, but nobody seemed to know what to actually do with the data. I decided to start talking to the analyst who was operating the system. I quickly noticed he was an extremely intelligent man.

Nonetheless, our conversation did not go smoothly. He kept on telling me what data points were available. 'Look at that connection with the retail information. We can visualise things,' he said. But every time I asked him how we could put this data to use, he told me that was an inappropriate question. That deeply puzzled me. I did not understand what he meant.

So I went on to talk to the marketers. They had heard that the data warehouse could do great things, that the data warehouse had lots of connections. But they were not using the data, because they didn't know what to do with it. How could this have happened? After a week, I decided to get rid of the entire data warehouse, since it was only costing us money.

I now understand what was going on back then, and I see the same problem in a lot of organisations: There is small analytical group that understands the power of data. They receive a budget, lock themselves up in a room with other specialists, and come out a few months later, telling the business they have this cool thing that will improve the company. But the business is too busy selling stuff, visiting clients, and producing the product. The business is disconnected. And because these business people have trusted their gut for so many years, they will not change their inner compass just because some nerds say they know better about the business and clients. So we threw out an entire data warehouse only to build a new one years later, this time run by business people.

—Xavier van Leeuwe

This example shows the classic gap between business and IT, between the analytical and the practical. If we take a step back, we can see what is happening here. Analysts like to talk about the data architecture, the variables, and the connections. They tend to focus on the *what*. Some analysts take it one step further and come closer to the *why*. They generate insights and pursue finding one singular truth: *Why is this happening?* Once they know why, they are satisfied. This is the reason many analysts are enthusiastic about what an organisation can *learn* from data—because they derive energy from the insight itself. But that is not good enough. We want to know what data can *do* for the business.

CENTRALISED DATA DEPARTMENT VERSUS DECENTRALISED DATA TEAM

There are two ways to design a data-driven organisation: One is to build a centralised data department. This will bring great benefits. It will be very efficient because it allows for specialised analysts: one for data architecture, one for database building, one for reporting, one for descriptive analysis, one for predictive analysis (which requires more statistical skills), and another for visualisation. You can put the best of the best on each aspect of the work. You avoid politics around data ownership, and definitions are the same for the whole company.

Centralised data teams, however, tend to focus on the wrong things, because the Achilles heel of any central data department is its communication (or lack thereof) with the rest of the business. These teams of highly intelligent people can be so disconnected from the real business issues that they can produce things that are considered unsolicited advice at best. A good analyst can predict who will stop a subscription with something called a *predictive churn model*. But if there is no concrete action by the business to prevent these people from actually stopping—like contacting them or sending a gift—nothing is improved. Some analysts seem to believe that having the analytical model alone will improve performance, but that is a common pitfall of data analysis. Many forget that insights are worthless if you do not turn them into better products, more effective campaigns, or better experiences for your customers. Centralised data teams can produce analyses very efficiently, but if there is no action attached, there won't be any impact.

There is another way to put data analysis at the heart of an organisation. At NRC, we found some intrinsically motivated business people with analytical minds and asked them to lead the data teams. They had been conditioned to aim for impact for the company because most of the time they were rewarded based on their results, and they received daily reports about sales, financials, conversions, or other business metrics. They mastered so-called 'contextual knowledge' and knew the business issues that kept top management awake at night.[5]

To find these kinds of leaders, watch for analytical people amongst project managers, marketers, and salespeople. What are they doing after work? What did they study? Once you've found a good candidate, we suggest you take that giant leap. Put an analytical businessperson in charge of the data team, and keep them extremely close to (preferably inside) the business teams. If these kinds of data teams are truly empowered and feel the freedom to follow their own course, they will start learning how they can

5   Thomas H. Davenport, one of the leading thinkers on incorporating business intelligence and analytics in organisations, puts forward that this kind of knowledge is essential for effective use of data ("Data to Knowledge to Results: Building an Analytical Capability," 2001).

implement their insights in the business, ask the right questions, and transform these questions into actionable insights. It is this last step that adds value.

These decentralised data specialists are like one-man armies: 'data Rambos,' one telecom analyst calls them. They are not experts in every field of analysis, but they can handle the basics of every part of the field and will make sure they are very effective. Their unique knowledge is developed within the company, which can provide a competitive edge.

The challenge with this approach is getting business people to learn about data and analytics. Marketers or sales representatives are not used to working with relational databases or thinking about reporting, data visualisation, or predictive analytics. When you start working with data, it's necessary to know how the data is generated and to learn the lingo of IT: the databases, the software solutions, and the people. If IT and business build a relationship, the company will reap the benefits of this mutual understanding for a long time to come.

2. RETHINK KPIS

On my first day at NRC, my manager introduced me to the company. After a brief explanation about the coffee machine and a chat about the weekend, he showed me my desk. It was settled in a nice corner in the marketing department, surrounded by my new colleagues.

And there it was, on the wall, just behind my new desk: a bold statement, printed on a piece of A3 paper, saying 'HOI + 1'. Because hoi *means* hello *in Dutch, I thought it was some kind of office joke. So I asked my manager what it meant. First he started laughing, then looked a little bit puzzled. He looked at me as if he was wondering whether he had made the right choice hiring me.*

On the same day, I found out that HOI is the name of the standard used by the Dutch audit bureau for newspaper circulation and that the marketing department at NRC had one—and only one—Key Performance Indicator (KPI): There had to be growth in circulation, as defined by the audit bureau statements. Because the overall market was declining, growth of only a single newspaper copy would be satisfying. There had to be a green number in the quarterly audit bureau publications.

At that moment, it made complete sense to me. With newspapers, it's always about circulation. When circulation is going up, more people read the paper, impact on society is growing, reach is growing, and advertisers will pay more for ads. Circulation was the main KPI for every newspaper in the Netherlands and for many around the world—and had been, for ages and ages.

—Matthijs van de Peppel

WRONG KPIs MAKE YOU DO STRANGE THINGS

Every industry has its own, unique version of audience measurement. In television they go on and on about the Nielsen ratings; the online industry is obsessed with comScore. In the news industry, it has always been audit bureau circulation. But are these the KPIs helping to grow the business?

For many years, the audit bureau was the guidance for daily working life at NRC. Everybody worked his or her hands to the bones for a little growth in the official-audience measurement. But to be honest, the singular focus on that metric made us do strange things.

Because we were so focused on growth in circulation (as calculated by the audit bureau standard), every single marketing promotion had to result in extra paper out of the printing house. That was the main goal of what we did. We did not really care if anybody actually wanted the newspaper. Sometimes we even pushed stuff on people who didn't want it, just to grow the official numbers. Here are four examples of bad decisions we made because of the focus on audience-measurement standards.

At NRC, it was possible to get a two-day subscription, with home delivery of just the Friday and Saturday newspaper. Subscribers who chose this product probably did so for a reason. But we, being clever marketing guys, just gave them an extra day. We told these customers, 'Your subscription will be extended. From now on, you will get the paper on Thursday as well. We are sure you will love it. In the first couple of months, you don't have to pay for it. Enjoy!' Nothing illegal happened, but it was a bad decision because many customers were offended.

Another example is the reward for sales agents. The full six-day product[6] would bring in a very nice bonus—much higher than for a weekend subscription—because it meant more paper out of the factory, which in turn was good for audit bureau standards. You can imagine what happened. With the higher bonus in mind, sales agents were pushing the six-day subscriptions no matter what. Even if potential subscribers told salespeople that they only wanted to

---

6   In the Netherlands, newspapers are published six days a week; there is no Sunday newspaper.

read the paper on weekends, the agent would tell them, 'This is a killer deal, just throw those unread weekday papers in the dustbin.'

Sometimes, we were even hurting our very valuable, loyal subscribers. We made it as hard as possible to temporarily pause delivery when on holiday. We hid the pausing option on the website and started asking an administrative fee of ten euros. That stopped many from pausing delivery, which was good for the official audience numbers. But at the same time, many subscribers complained that they had to pay us for *not* delivering the newspaper.

Last but not least, we delivered our newspaper to people who were not really interested. We used the amazing power of *free*. You could get our newspaper for free, on trial. A lot of people will take anything when the word *free* is involved,[7] so this looked like quite a successful way to get more paper out of the printing house.

With the benefit of hindsight, it seems clear that these actions don't make sense. The voice of the customer is completely ignored, and you don't have to be a professor in statistics to predict that this kind of behaviour will backfire in the long term. And backfire it did. One third of the two-day subscribers stopped because they didn't want a third day pushed down their throat. The newly acquired six-day customers stopped as soon as their contract ended because they were tired of throwing away five newspapers a week. The free trials didn't take root and were actually costing us money due to acquisition cost and variable printing and distribution costs. Finally, loyal readers who didn't want to pay for the holiday service just ended their subscription before they went on vacation. Many times, they didn't reactivate after their holiday and were lost.

---

7   Dan Ariely, *Predictably Irrational* (New York: HarperCollins, 2008).

Maybe the weirdest thing of all is that it took us years to realise that these actions were not helping the company. Because circulation was going up, official audience-measurement numbers were green, graphs on the wall were going the right way, and editors were cheering. Everybody was happy.

It was only after a couple of years, when we realised we were running out of tricks to inflate circulation numbers, that we started to question the objective on the wall: 'HOI + 1'.

FIND KPIs THAT REPRESENT COMPANY HEALTH

When this brutal realisation struck us, we had to rethink our one and only KPI. Was it really true that circulation was the one thing that drove our newspaper business? We came to the conclusion that this was not the case, because when we drive a lot of newspapers out of the printing house, that doesn't necessarily mean we are earning a lot of money in the long term. It does not mean that people are reading those papers. The correlation between paper circulation and company health was only true in the old days, when everybody had the same six-day subscription and was paying the full price.

These days, circulation can consist of a lot of different kinds of subscriptions with a lot of different margins. A full-price weekend subscription brings in a lot more money than a 'five weeks for ten euros' trial subscription, but in terms of circulation numbers, the trial for the full week is six times better than full price for the Saturday.

In the old days, more paper out of the factory meant more reach and more advertising money. Nowadays, the sad truth is that advertising income is down for newspapers when circulation is down *and* when circulation is up. The correlation is weak.

So we waved goodbye to our one and only KPI, which had driven our company since 1828. Then we started the hardest part: defining new KPIs. We sat in a room for hours, asking ourselves, 'What is really driving the value of this company, when it's not circulation, as defined by the audit bureau?' We tried to frame it into a golden rule that is simple and always works.[8]

We couldn't get away with just saying we needed a healthy financial margin, mostly expressed in EBITDA (earnings before interest, taxes, depreciation, and amortisation). That makes perfect sense, but you can't tell a marketing department to go out and earn some EBITDA. So what's below the surface?

That's where we came up with *relationships*. The real value in our company comes from the relationships we are building with our readers. And those relationships have to be real. It doesn't count if you push the newspaper into a letterbox and nothing happens. It has to be a serious, two-sided relationship, just like the ones you cherish in your personal life.

From that perspective, the term *core relationship* was born. A core relationship has a positive value both for the customer and for the company. The calculation is simple: Count all your subscribers as one subscriber. Don't divide a Saturday subscription by six, as many circulation audit bureaus do. And don't count subscriptions with higher costs than revenue, like trials that stop automatically.

---

8   After reading Jim Collins book Good to Great (2001), we used his idea of the *hedgehog principle*.

KPIs DRIVE CULTURE

The change seems to be very subtle. Core relationships or circulation—it's just another calculation of the same thing. But the impact on the company has been huge. The change in weekly reporting did all the work and changed the organisational culture. From the moment we started to report on core relationships, the mind-set started to shift. The marketing department, traditionally driven by the sales charts of the day, started to worry about building relationships with new and current subscribers.

All of a sudden, our call centre was more interesting than any other department. We saw its true potential. The employees there were building relationships with our subscribers all day long. We wanted to get rid of stupid rules instead of hurting our customers with annoying fees or subpar service. *Every* individual subscriber counted, not just the six-day customer, who accounted for more in audit-bureau measurement. The holiday service became free of charge, and we started to promote it in the newspaper and with e-mails. Bonuses for sales agents became equal for every form of core subscription. Like Starbucks, we introduced our own kind of LATTE system for sales reps.[9] We asked them to **listen** to customers, **acknowledge** their needs, **take** action by selling the subscription that fits their lives, **thank** them, and **explain** what the further steps are. This reduced cancellations and increased long-term retention.

We started to look for patterns in the data about what kinds of products or promotions were building real relationships. For the first time, we analysed what happened after a subscriber came in. It

---

9   Charles Duhigg, *The Power of Habit* (New York: Random House, 2012).

turned out that twenty thousand customers per year change their subscription because their current package doesn't fit their needs anymore. We also found that the acquired weekend subscribers stayed much longer than the full-week subscribers because a single newspaper per week was just better for their busy lives.

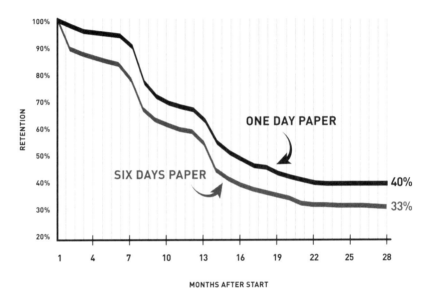

Retention analysis shows more loyalty from customers who chose a subscription with one paper. However, for the audit bureau, the six-day paper subscription counted for six times more circulation, attracting our focus but going against customer needs.

Sales numbers were also not as clear as they seemed. Because of the pushy behaviour of the sales agents, over 10 per cent of subscribers cancelled their order within a month. We started to understand how we could listen to our customers through the data. If six-day subscriptions had a lower retention rate, then we had sold the wrong subscription in the first place. We hadn't listened properly to customers' needs.

In summary, the new KPI started a culture in which we listened to what our customers wanted instead of trying to enforce what we needed. And from then on, we worked our hands to the bone to optimise customer experience and grow the number of core relationships. We started thinking of the longer term. How do we maximise the number of healthy relationships? It wasn't by endlessly hunting for new relationships but instead by making existing customers happy. To do this, we had to understand their needs. The table below illustrates how a new KPI drives a cultural change in many parts of an organisation.

	CIRCULATION ACCORDING TO AUDIT BUREAU	RELATIONSHIPS
KEY METRICS	sales, revenue per transaction	retention, lifetime value
EMPLOYEES	order takers, driven by senior management's needs	customer-success agents, driven by customer needs
MOTIVATION	salary	fulfilling a mission by meeting human needs
INTERACTIONS	minimal: send the product	critical: listen, touch base regularly
WAY OF WORKING	silo based	cooperation across silos
FOCUS	self, vertical, internal, today	other, horizontal, external, next year
SUPPORT	minimise handling times, resolve incidents	sincere attention, help use product more efficiently
BRANDING	ad campaigns	word of mouth
REWARD SYSTEM	transaction, quantity	lifetime value, quality
ACQUISITION	always be closing, no thresholds, wide funnel, push what you want to sell	attract right customers, engage, motivate ambassadorship, intelligent threshold, chute, ask what customer wants

New KPI leads to new culture.

BITE THE BULLET

At the same time, some dramatic things happened to our circulation numbers in HOI. We stopped selling automatically stopping trials, because our data told us that these were not building real relationships (much more on this later). So after a couple of weeks, a huge trial bubble burst, and we lost tens of thousands in the audience-measurement standards.

We knew this was going to happen, and we were quite sure that it wouldn't really hurt our company financially, because automatically stopping trials had a negative value. But beyond a group of insiders, there were hundreds of employees and people outside the business who were not aware of the change in policy. And how could they have been? Even if we had told them with press releases and memos stating, 'We changed our KPIs', it takes a while for every person to say goodbye to a 189-year-old legacy—especially if your newspaper is the only one in the Netherlands to stop selling trials, and it is imploding in the quarterly industry reports.

So we had to bite a very big bullet. The editorial department questioned the capacities of the circulation department. How could the best newspaper in the country have the worst circulation numbers? That is why you need top-management support. In every market and at every company, the ride will be bumpy if you introduce new KPIs at the expense of the figures the rest of the company grew up with. You will need a very strong umbrella to protect you from the heavy rains pouring down.

NEW KPIs IN YOUR INDUSTRY

This story is mainly driven by occurrences in the newspaper business, but the lessons can be just as useful in other industries. When you start to look carefully at the KPIs around you, you will definitely notice that some strange things are going on. For example, at some online shops, daily reports show the top ten products sold, without revenue or margin. These kinds of reports make marketers think that successful products are the products with high sales numbers, so they start hunting for these numbers by selling cheap stuff with a lousy margin.

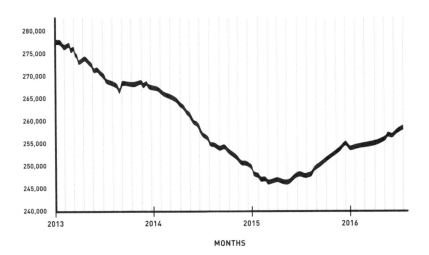

NRC core relationships 2013–2016.

One of our business partners from Data Sherpa, Jimmy de Vreede, points out that retail companies often solely look at revenue, volume, and margin when delisting a product and forget the customer behind the product. A product with low margin and volume might have a profitable customer base that buys a lot more than the one product. By delisting one product based on the wrong KPIs, a store risks losing customers who visit the store for that single unprofitable product whilst also putting other products in the shopping cart.

KPIs drive organisational cultures all around you and reveal how businesses are managed. Dare to ask yourself if the KPIs you use are the core drivers of value for your financials and your customers. If they are not, figure out which KPIs are the right ones, and don't hesitate to change systems, data, reports, and analyses. You will be amazed by the impact. Just don't forget your umbrella.

3. PUNCH THROUGH THE BIG DATA HYPE

In the past few years, there has been a lot of talk about big data. *At almost every conference and in many boards and marketing departments, the idea rose that the Holy Grail was knowing everything about everybody at every moment. I was no exception. Developing holistic user profiles was on top of my priority list.*

Then, one weekend, I visited my parents. Now and then, in their little village in the Dutch countryside, they make a brave attempt to understand how my brothers and I fill our working days. So I tried to explain my new project to collect as much individual data from subscribers and website visitors as possible—how we wanted to know much more than how to contact them and where to deliver the newspaper. What do they read? What is their income, their number of kids, their educational level, their birthday, their interests, the computer brand they use? We wanted all the personal information we could get our hands on to build profiles of them—everything from everybody, really.

At one point, my mother shyly asked, 'Maybe I just don't understand, but why does my newspaper have to know all that stuff from me? I don't really like you to know everything from me. It feels a little intrusive.' With that simple question—as she had many times before—my mother made sure that both my legs were firmly on the ground.

—Matthijs van de Peppel

THE POWER OF BIG DATA

So what is *big data*? A common way to define the border between *regular data* and *big data* is the three Vs:[10]

- Volume: the amount of data is large.

- Variety: the data is often not clean and tabular but is messy, like text or images.

- Velocity: new data arrives continuously.

In the publishing world, we usually speak about big data when combining online behaviour (like clicks and scrolls) and offline data (like names and addresses). There is some amazing software

---

10   Doug Laney, "3D Data Management: Controlling Data Volume, Velocity and Variety," *META Group*, BibSonomy, February 2001.

available to collect, combine, and report all this data. In section 4, you can see what analytical tools, such as Mather Listener, can do.

Every company has the opportunity to collect huge amounts of data from its customers. That feeds the imagination, but what can you actually do with it? Here are some examples:

PERSONALISED PRODUCTS

By knowing your individual customers' interests, habits, and personal situations, you can match your digital products to their needs. Not everybody has to see the same homepage on your website, for example. Sports fans could get a different landing page than politics aficionados.

TARGETED ADS

Yes, Facebook has finally entered our story. It is earning large amounts of money with targeted advertising. Facebook probably knows more about its customers than any other company in the history of mankind because that's what it's primarily used for—sharing as much as possible about yourself. Facebook gives advertisers the opportunity to target campaigns at almost every imaginable segment of demographics and interests. Advertisers are investing big sums to reach exactly the audience they want to reach. Almost any traditional publisher dreams of this kind of advertising money.

DATA MINING

One of the most intriguing possibilities of big data is the chance to find hidden gems in your data. It goes like this: you store all the data you can get and drag it into the Amazon cloud, even before you have the slightest idea of what you will do with it. The magic comes when you start data mining. Algorithms can find patterns in the data that you never could have foreseen. This kind of analysis is used, for example, to find correlations between DNA strings and the rate of success of certain medicines. It can also be used, for example, to find drivers for churn (stops).

PREDICTIVE MODELLING AND MACHINE LEARNING

If your algorithms find correlations between certain variables in data, the next step is to make predictions. For example, knowing which series will be popular is a great feat by Netflix's data team. Medical researchers understand what medicine will have the best chances of success on particular patients based on their DNA. Telecom companies better understand which subscribers are likely to churn. These predictions can be automatically generated, and the predictive model can improve itself via machine learning.

CASE STUDY
CUSTOMER ENGAGEMENT AFFECTS RETENTION

OBJECTIVE: A publisher wanted to understand how digital engagement with their content affected retention of their subscribers.

APPROACH: Data on site traffic was collected and matched to customer account information. Subscribers receive unlimited access to content on digital platforms (both browsers and mobile devices) in addition to print copies of the product. Those customers who activated their digital access were identified, and their content consumption was measured to track their engagement. The site traffic data was captured using a tagging solution and stored in a cloud-based data warehouse. The raw site traffic data was aggregated by customer and matched to customer account data from the billing system.

RESULTS: Customer activity was tracked for six months. Customers who had activated their digital access and consumed content digitally at least once per week were observed to have 91 per cent retention. Customers who had activated their digital access but were infrequent users of digital content had 88 per cent retention, and customers who had not activated their digital access had a retention rate of 84 per cent. Controlling for other customer attributes using statistically valid samples for test groups, digital engagement was found to have a significant positive effect on customer retention. Based on these findings, the publisher initiated a content-promotion campaign designed to encourage online registration and promote digital engagement.

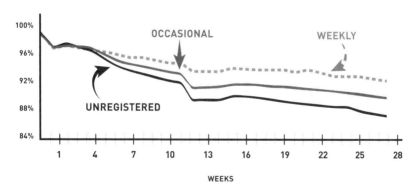

This is retention data by week for three groups of subscribers: 1) those that had not activated their digital access to content (unregistered) 2) those that had activated their access but were infrequent users of digital content, and 3) those that had activated their access and were frequent users of digital content.

USE BIG DATA WITH COMMON SENSE

There are all these applications of big data, and storing data gets cheaper and easier every day. This combination shapes a lot of opportunities for new and existing companies. Consultancies pop up like fair maids in spring, software is developed at a rapid speed, and no week goes by without an e-mail hitting our inboxes from some company with a state-of-the-art big-data solution. There is a new, pretty girl in town, and she keeps asking for a date. That's hard to resist.

But the thing is, this girl is not right for everybody. Big data is not equally relevant to every company, and building up holistic user profiles is probably not the thing to start with if you are turning into a data-driven company.

Before you start investing in Hadoop clusters, cloud storage, machine-learning algorithms, and a lot of expensive and scarce manpower, try to bring common sense into the equation and ask yourself if these investments will pay off at some point in the future. Are your customers interested in a personalised product? Are your advertisers interested in hypersegmentation? What are the chances you will find patterns in your data that will earn you serious money? And last, but definitely not least, what will your relationships think of you when you tell them what kind of data you are collecting about them? How do you feel about that?

If you have a solid business case for your big-data project, the next question should be, what data is really needed here? Is it important to know 'everything from everybody', or will a couple of data points do the job?

We were facing these questions at NRC, after Matthijs' sobering visit to his parents. The first step we took was visiting companies we had befriended in other industries who were far ahead of us on this path, to find out if their extensive customer profiles brought golden insights.

We reached out and received a lot of enthusiasm. Many companies were willing to share their experiences and show their systems. We saw amazing Hadoop installations, many terabytes of personal data, and many analysts, data scientists, and business developers who had invested serious time and money in big data. We asked only one question: Can you tell us your million-dollar business case for big data? Because after these investments, there has to be at least one application of big data that had a big payoff, right?

Despite the transparency, success cases where quite scarce, and the connection between those successes and the big-data projects was weak. For example, there was a case involving a home-decoration store. They had an impressive loyalty programme that brought them huge amounts of data about their customers and their purchases. What you buy should say a lot about the stage of your life you are in—about how you live—so there are endless opportunities for analysis of that data. But it was not possible for this store to attribute a clear profit to having all that data about customers.

When we persisted, there turned out to be one particular thing that really paid off for the home-decoration store, and it was a lot simpler than we expected. The store sent an e-mail and asked what the customers were planning to renovate in the next couple of months. When customers told them that they are planning, for example, to rebuild the bathroom, the company would send offers on bathroom tiles, showers, and taps. Response rates went through the roof.

That was the million-dollar business case. But it was not very complicated. It was one question and one answer—not what you would call *big data*. The data volume is small, the data has low variety, and it does not come in continuously—it is just one data point through e-mail.

None of the firms at the forefront of data usage we met were able to share examples showing that the holistic profiles of their customers really paid off. 'But', one analyst told us, 'It's a great toy!'

DON'T DO BIG DATA FOR THE SAKE OF BIG DATA

Maybe that's the risk of the big-data hype. Most people in the boardroom don't really know how these data projects work, but almost all agree they should 'do something with big data' because that's what they hear at conferences and read in management books. For those who do know how big data works, this new era is a dream come true. There is money, fancy software, support from top management, and more data than ever. It's like a planet-sized playground where you can play for ages. So if we lose common sense about data, chances are that companies are 'doing big data' not for the business but just for the sake of big data.

As we wrote in chapter 1, it helps when business people lead the data teams. They will make business cases and evaluate whether the investment in time and money is justified by the predicted earnings in money or improved customer experience. If it is justified, go for it, keeping in mind that you have to start by doing three things: comply with privacy legislation, keep the relationship with your customers in mind, and be sure you understand your basic business processes before you start a big-data project.

PRIVACY LEGISLATION

There are big differences in privacy laws around the world. For example, people in the United States seem to have less concern about lost personal privacy than Europeans do. Americans may more readily accept that data capture occurs and that companies use information on demographics and behaviours for a variety of purposes. There are Americans who actively try to thwart data-collection attempts, but they are a very small part of the market. Americans may trust companies with their data to a greater degree than they trust their government.

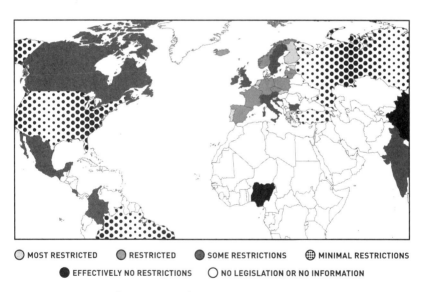

MOST RESTRICTED   RESTRICTED   SOME RESTRICTIONS   MINIMAL RESTRICTIONS
EFFECTIVELY NO RESTRICTIONS   NO LEGISLATION OR NO INFORMATION

Data privacy heat map (Forrester, 2015)

Europeans appear to trust their governments with their data but take a wary eye towards data capture by the private sector. Privacy protection is a hot topic, legislation is strict, and regulatory agencies are active and powerful. Building a profile of customers without telling them exactly what information you store and what you are going to do with it is forbidden by the European Union.[11] More practical information about dealing with privacy in customer analytics is described in section 4.

STEP IN YOUR CUSTOMER'S SHOES

Besides the question of whether a big-data project will bring value to your business, there is also an ethical question to ask. To what extent do you store, connect, and analyse the personal data of your customers? If you are in the relationship business, you may want to be careful with the collection of knowledge about your partners.

If you decide that you want to know 'everything from everybody', ask yourself how you would feel if you found out that your wife or husband wanted to know everything from you at every moment. What if your partner tracked your phone, analysed your spending behaviour, and read your e-mails without letting you know? It would cause serious doubts about the trust and equality in the relationship.

At NRC, we have become very cautious in what we do with the personal data of our customers and website visitors. We always ask ourselves two questions before we start any big-data project: Is there a positive business case? And can we explain to our mothers that we use this data?

---

11   By European regulation on personal data, which comes into force in 2018.

Another future option will be to put the customer in the driver seat. Tools will be developed to empower customers to control the flow, use of their personal data, and dictate their own terms of service.[12]

CASE STUDY

WHAT DATA SHOULD BE CAPTURED?

OBJECTIVE: A publisher wanted to develop a predictive model to support customer-acquisition campaign design and targeting. They sought to understand which product offers and customer attributes were important determinants of offer acceptance. The model findings would help the publisher design the acquisition offers and target the prospective customers most likely to accept the offers.

APPROACH: Mather Economics designed a model of customer-acceptance rates using a field of econometrics called *discrete choice models*. To accurately predict outcomes, the model needed to include factors that were important to the customer's decision. If some important factors were omitted, the model's predictions could be biased and inaccurate.

The terms included in the model were product-offer characteristics, customer attributes, seasonality patterns, and macroeconomic factors. Product-offer characteristics included price per month, subscription term, automatic payment via credit

---

12   Doc Searls, *The Intention Economy* (Boston: Harvard Business Review Press, 2012).

card, and the length of the promotion period. Customer attributes included age group, income level, gender, presence of children in the household, and subscriptions to other periodicals. Seasonality and macroeconomic factors were represented by time variables such as month of offer and the Dow Jones average.

Mather Economics determined that these variables were the *relevant* data for the purpose of the analysis. Omitting customer attributes or other important data would make the model ineffective and unreliable, as these factors play important roles in predicting the acceptance rates of the offers. Sometimes the necessary data are not obvious until the modelling process begins and initial findings are obtained.

RESULTS: A reliable, accurate model of customer acquisition was developed using data from prior acquisition campaigns. The model produced predicted acceptance rates for prospective customers, and the prospects were prioritised for campaign targeting. After testing the approach, the data feeds and list-generation process were automated for ongoing operations. Using this targeting approach increased the acceptance rates for direct mail campaigns by 40 per cent.

4. START WITH THE BASICS

Just a couple of years ago we were in a room with three people—an analyst, a marketer, and a data warehouse developer—and we discussed a question that looked very simple on first sight: 'What is a subscription?'

We got three different answers. The marketer was counting in terms of the audit bureau standard (Saturday-only delivery is divided by six), as the new KPI had not sunk in yet. The data warehouse developer counted the pieces of the package in the subscription system (digital as one, the newspaper as one), and the analyst wanted to count the bundles regardless of frequency in delivery and number of pieces in the system. Not being able to agree about this single question was very confounding. We had to nail down these very basic definitions of our business for the brand new data warehouse.

—Matthijs van de Peppel

So, now you have a data team led by business people, but you don't want to start with a big-data project. What can you do?

We found that when trying to understand day-to-day business, there is a lot of work to do with the relatively small amounts of structured data already available in the current systems. It turned out there were a lot more basics than we thought, and we had to define many metrics before we could start to report and analyse them. What is a new subscriber? When is an ex-subscriber a prospect? When is a new subscription a switcher? What is the revenue per subscription? What are the variable costs? How many paying customers do we have, and at what price? [13]

We basically didn't understand what was really happening with the 260,000 relationships we had. That's strange because at the same time, we were telling each other that those relationships were the one thing bringing value to the company.

So we chose to invest time and money in developing definitions, data preparation in our data warehouse, and reports on the basics in our business-intelligence tool. These are not the sexiest subjects for data analysts and scientists. They're not big-data toys. It's not Hadoop; it's just counting 260,000 records and their evolution. But at the same time, this is exactly what paid off.

We started to see how many core relationships we had, as well as which promotions and products were driving the relationships and which were bad for relationships. We understood what kind of service kept the relationships alive. After a while, we went from

---

13   Davenport (2013) calls this kind of descriptive analysis on basic business processes 'Analytics 1.0', as opposed to 'Analytics 2.0' and 'Analytics 3.0', which contain big-data methods like predictive and prescriptive modelling.

reporting the past to forecasting the future and started to understand the buttons we could push to improve results.[14] More than a year after that confounding meeting where we were not able to count our subscribers, the improvements started to pay off, and we started to grow in terms of both relationships and our financial bottom line.

It is advisable to start with the basics. Maybe this doesn't sound very new or revolutionary. When you build a house, you start with the foundation—not with a carport. For some reason, that's not how it usually goes in the field of data science. Many analysts will choose the sexy big-data projects and skip the basics. It's like asking a mechanic if he wants to change the tires of a car or tune the engine.

BASIC	ADVANCED	EXPERT

· defining KPIs
· reporting
  □ financials
  □ volume
  □ upsell and downsell
· list management
· funnel analysis
· return on marketing investment
· online A/B testing
	· revenue forecasting
	· volume forecasting
	· retention analysis
	· customer lifetime value (CLV) projection
	· segmentation
	· identifying drivers of turnover
	· price-elasticity analysis
	· individual employee performance
		· customer profiles
		· propensity to buy
		· propensity to stop (churn)
		· data mining
		· process mining
		· next-best offer prediction
		· online tracking of individuals
		· real-time dashboards
		· behaviour-based advertising

Stages in data expertise for marketing purposes[15]

14   In section 4, we include more information on revenue forecasting.

15   Adapted from Datasherpa.

REMEMBER

- When it comes to analytics, put business people in the lead.

- Put data people directly in the business teams.

- Dare to question your KPIs: Are these the drivers of real value?

- KPIs can change culture and drive success.

- Don't do big data just for the sake of big data.

- Only start data projects with a positive business case.

- There's an ethical threshold for storing data.

- Understand local privacy regulations.

- The first extra millions are probably in understanding the basics of your business.

SECTION 2.

BUILD VALUABLE RELATIONSHIPS

After building the data teams and using the right data, it becomes important to put your findings to use so your organisation or business can grow. Only when a relationship is beneficial for both your customers and the company will the organisation prevail. This section explains how you can use data to attract the right customers—ones who are willing to commit to a longer-term relationship—and how you can keep those relationships going by understanding the influence of pricing.

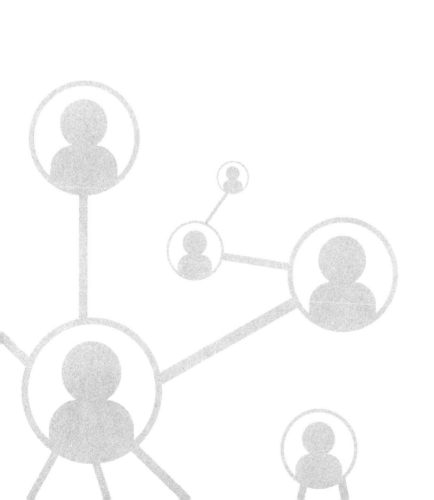

5. DON'T BREAK UP
OVER MONEY

It's July, and it's pricing time. The CEO, CFO, CMO, editor-in-chief, and I are gathered for our yearly ritual. The CFO leads off: 'Okay, let's start with our six-day sub-scription, how much did we raise that one last year?'

'2.3 per cent', says the CMO.

CEO: 'What was the inflation this year?'

CMO: '2.1 per cent.'

CEO: 'Okay, let's do 2.6 per cent this year. A little bit over inflation.'

The editor-in-chief joins the conversation. 'No, I don't like that, the yearly price would get above 400. Subscribers might stop for that reason. And besides that, our competi-tor didn't raise that much last year.'

CFO: 'Okay, let's do 2.2 per cent, to keep the yearly price just under 400 euros.'

CEO: 'Agreed. Next product.'

I was filling out my Excel files and saw millions of euros flying back and forth. Decisions about the future health of customer relationships and the future of our company were made in seconds, purely on gut feeling. We didn't have a clue how these decisions would turn out. How many subscribers would stop when we raised prices by 2.2 per cent, or with a hypothetical 10 per cent? Were customers really comparing prices with our competitors? Was our brand too weak to resist a lower price offered by our competition?

The inner workings of the pricing machine were a complete mystery to us until Mather Economics crossed our path, and then everything changed. We were a complete mystery to us until we were introduced to price-elasticity analysis. This showed us that it's possible to determine price sensitivity. With these tools, we can predict how many lost subscribers will result from any given price increase. And from that moment onwards, the gut was not shaping our future: the data was.

—*Matthijs van de Peppel*

FIND YOUR BALANCE

Price-elasticity analysis is an incredibly powerful instrument to help lead your business where you want it to go. When marketing teams understand the impact of prices, they can determine whether they want a lot of customers for a smaller amount of money per capita, or if they want to pursue a strategy with fewer customers who are each paying a lot more (or anything in between). In section 4, different tools for pricing analysis and yield management are described in detail.

At NRC, we used price-elasticity modelling to grow the number of relationships without declining in total margin. Since we are a newspaper company, we like to see ourselves as fulfilling a mission. We are on Earth to stimulate development. We feel that our journalists balance the executive powers in our society. We can only fulfil this mission if there are enough people reading what we write. A hypothetical newspaper company with only one reader paying the entire yearly turnover would be financially healthy, but it won't play a significant role in society.

Understanding the impact of pricing can be used to make more money per customer. Sometimes this implies having fewer customers paying you more money, using large price hikes. Pricing analysis can also be used to prevent vulnerable customers from stopping after a price increase, thus obtaining the maximum amount of customers.

ANALYSE REAL BEHAVIOUR

In our experience, and somewhat contradictorily, it is not very helpful to ask customers what they would do at a certain price level or what price they think is reasonable. It appears that when it comes to the value of a certain product or service, customers are clueless.[16]

Let's do a mental experiment to illustrate this. Imagine you are walking through a flea market in an old European city, and you are attracted to a wooden lamp. It looks nice and has an artistic touch to it. The lamp would fit perfectly in your living room, so you walk up to the guy selling it. Now imagine two scenarios:

1. The guy tells you he just moved in with his girlfriend. The wooden lamp was in his dorm. He bought it five years ago at IKEA.

2. He tells you the lamp belonged to an artist who just passed away. In his workshop, he had this wooden lamp from the fifties, handmade by a famous Danish designer.

Most people end up paying a lot more for this lamp in the Danish-designer scenario than in the IKEA scenario, despite the fact that the material, quality, and design of the lamp haven't changed. These are the effects of mental accounting, extensively researched by Richard Thaler.[17]

The only way to find out how people really respond to different price points is by testing in real life. It is ideal to use control groups, which receive no price increase, compared to others who do. By measuring the difference in lost customers between the control group and the others, it is possible to define the impact of price changes for different customers and different products.

---

16   William Poundstone, *Priceless: The Myth of Fair Value (and How to Take Advantage of It)* (New York: Hill and Wang, 2010).

17   Richard Thaler, "Mental accounting and consumer choice," *Marketing Science* 4 (1985): 199–214.

What we found at NRC was remarkable. Different forms of subscriptions turned out to have huge differences in price sensitivity. For some products, a small increase caused a tsunami of extra cancellations. On the other side of the spectrum, there seemed to be products where double-digit increases didn't have any effect on retention.

This information gives fantastic insights about the exact value customers attach to your product. This is quite spectacular because those same people would not have been able to tell you if you asked them.

INCREASE PRICES WITH MINIMAL STRAIN

In almost every recurring revenue-based business, price increases every once in awhile are inevitable because costs increase due to inflation. At the same time, an increase in subscription price can be a reason for customers to stop their subscriptions and leave the company without any income from those people. Every company with recurring income should pay a lot of attention to finding the balance between increasing prices and, at the same time, preventing customers from stopping their subscriptions. Price-elasticity analysis does exactly that.

When we got insights on the price sensitivity of subscribers, we were able to adjust prices to protect the financial health of the company, but with a minimal impact on the number of relationships affected. We increased prices with minimal strain on groups of vulnerable customers, while the ones who could bear some burden had their prices increased accordingly. In this way, pricing analysis did a great job preventing 'break-ups'.

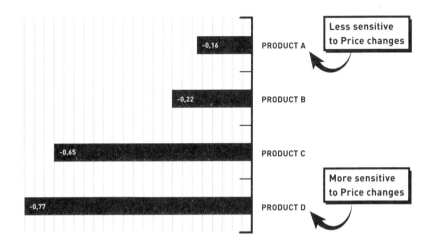

Price elasticity at NRC shows some products can handle price increases better than others. Price elasticity for product A is -0.16, which means that a +1 per cent price increase will result in a 0.16 per cent decrease in volume.

WHEN YOU TAKE THIS TO ANOTHER LEVEL

Being as smart as you are, you are probably connecting some dots right now. When you get granular and start analysing pricing, in theory it's possible to define prices on an individual level. This would give you even better results, because in the end, no two customers are the same. The decision on whether to differentiate pricing by customer, by product, or by any other metric is up to each organisation. NRC does not vary pricing by individual customer, but Mather Economics works with many organisations that successfully employ that strategy. There is more on segmented pricing in section 4.

CASE STUDY

HOW UNDERSTANDING PRICE ELASTICITY GENERATED $10 MILLION

OBJECTIVE: A large US publisher needed to increase audience revenue without increasing customer churn. They had annual price increases and wanted to understand price elasticity across their customer base to improve future yield.

APPROACH: Mather Economics estimated price elasticity using econometric models and developed a test-and-learn process using A/B testing, where two versions (A and B) are compared. The versions are identical except for one variation that might affect a user's behaviour, thus hinting to an optimised outcome. Mather developed survival models (which predict retention of customers over time) using past customer behaviour and estimated price elasticity for the publisher's current customers. Mather selected accounts for the target and control groups, suggested prices on a per-customer basis, tracked customer behaviour, and reported the weekly performance of the groups.

RESULTS: The test results showed that significant differences in price elasticity existed within the customer base. Important factors for predicting individual customers' price elasticity were their tenure, their digital engagement, and their product mix. Demographics, acquisition channel, geographic location, and several other factors were also found to have significant effects on price response. The A/B test results validated the econometric model predictions. Applying these insights to the annual price-increase process improved the yield by 40 per cent—approximately $10 million per year.

PRICE STOP % FROM 5% PRICE INCREASE

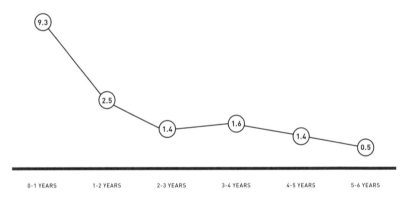

CUSTOMER ACTIVE LIFETIME

6. FIND THE RIGHT PRICE TO ATTRACT NEW CUSTOMERS

Like the gut-led discussion about price increases described in the previous chapter, NRC had a similar ritual for determining acquisition prices. Marketers would come together and offer their gut intuitions on the best pricing strategy. Because the marketers had targets for the number of new subscriptions to acquire in their own channels, each made a case for the best prices to be in their channel.

The online marketer would say that the website needs the best price because on the website there is no possibility for a direct conversation. At the same time, the marketer responsible for sales by telephone would argue that it would help if the sales agent could offer a better price than the one customers saw on the website. The people selling subscriptions on the streets said that it was difficult to grab the attention of shoppers and that they were in the windswept streets of the Netherlands rather than a comfortable office like the telesales reps, so obviously they needed a better acquisition price than the other channels. In the end we would balance all these interests and agree to a great number of propositions to shoot at potential subscribers. Gut instinct ruled the business again.

—Matthijs van de Peppel

To find the right price for new customers, start by taking gut instinct out of the equation. Together with Mather Economics, NRC gathered and analysed data about campaigns from the past years—literally hundreds of propositions, prices for many products offered to millions of prospects, and success rates. Statistics and a couple of very smart analysts predicted an optimal price point. It turned out to be scary and counterintuitive. For example, the product we sold the most was the Saturday hard-copy newspaper combined with digital access on weekdays. We offered it at €14.50

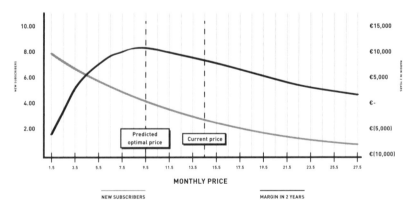

Statistical analysis points to lower acquisition price for bringing in more relationships and more revenue.

a month. The statistical model predicted an optimal price of €9. In theory, it would bring us thousands of new subscribers and lots of extra margin. This struck us as wrong because our gut told us that we had to *increase* the price to earn more money. Nobody would care about a couple of euros more a month for our great newspaper, we reckoned. Right?

GUT VERSUS STATISTICS

It's not easy to work with control groups and analyse the results in real-world, direct-marketing situations. There are always human sales agents involved who do or don't believe in a certain proposition and are frustrated because they feel they cannot offer the best deal in their channel. This human factor cannot be overlooked.

Luckily, we live in the age of the Internet. There is some great and affordable software out there that enables online A/B testing on real customers by splitting the traffic and showing them different versions of the website with different offers. We used these kinds of tests to measure the effect of different price levels on acquisition numbers.

We decided to test the gut against the model and defined a higher price (€17.50) and a lower price (€11.50) for the product. To compare the success of the two price points, we used two KPIs: the number of new subscribers and the forecasted customer lifetime value (CLV) of these subscribers in two years. Check out the data toolbox in section 4 for more information on how to calculate CLV.

We started with the gut price point and implemented the higher price on the website in an A/B test against the normal price. After four weeks, we had significant results showing a decline in conversion and a small gain in CLV margin projected over two years—no big surprises so far.

The more interesting experiment was the one with the lower price. While the model predicted big things from this change, we didn't believe it. We put the lower price on the website on a Wednesday, and even as soon as the next Monday, it was clear that something spectacular was happening. The number of new subscribers coming in almost doubled. After two weeks, results were significant, and we were left with a dazzling +81 per cent in new subscribers and +38 per cent in CLV.

We unleashed the power of analytics to build new relationships while improving company value at the same time. Our guts felt stupid.

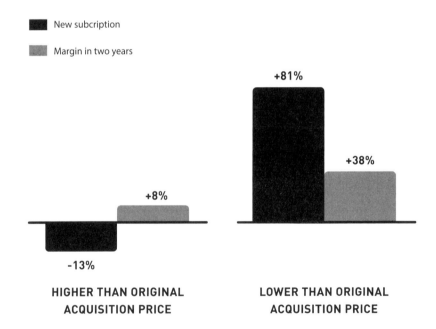

New subcription

Margin in two years

+81%

+38%

+8%

-13%

HIGHER THAN ORIGINAL
ACQUISITION PRICE

LOWER THAN ORIGINAL
ACQUISITION PRICE

A/B test: the right acquisition price brings more readers and more money.

7. STOP DATING, GET ENGAGED

In June of 2014, I gazed at the computer screen in disbelief. Was this really what we had been doing for so many years? I was looking at the first graphs from our recently built data warehouse. Up to that day, we hadn't been able to track customers beyond their initial subscription. Now we saw their lifetime behaviour, and it didn't look good. The trial subscriptions we had been hunting so ferociously for so many years plunged to nearly zero retention within a couple of months after conversion into regular subscriptions.

Was it really that bad? It was. One particular line, however, showed a retention rate after thirty months of seventy times higher than the trials. 'What are those?' I asked Matthijs. They turned out to be newspaper subscriptions that came with an iPad. The biannual contracts had nearly perfect retention for the first twenty-four months and saw a gentle slope afterwards. The slight downward slope was nowhere near the plunge the trials took.

The iPads were the subscriptions we were most worried of losing because all the outsiders were telling us that the customers just wanted the iPad and not our news. It turned out to be the exact opposite. Apparently this offer had attracted a special breed of customer. Somehow we had been able to establish a relationship with the majority of the newly acquired customers who chose the iPad offer. We were definitely not giving away iPads for free. The monthly payment was 30 per cent higher than a regular subscription. This threshold had attracted more valuable customers. It had attracted customers who were willing to build a relationship.

—*Xavier van Leeuwe*

NETFLIXISATION

Giving away free trials is a common practice for any industry that has little or no variable cost. Take software: Once you've programmed it, there is no cost if more people use it, and it makes sense to let customers try your actual product instead of investing in a big marketing budget to raise brand awareness. Trials maximise the exposure of products to potential consumers and minimise the consumers' uncertainty about quality.

Some industries that do suffer from substantial variable cost still employ trials. In those cases, there is usually a very high degree of competition or an obsession with short-term market share. In the case of the news industry in the Netherlands, two- to six-week trial subscriptions have been the gold standard for many years. Customers have become fully accustomed and expect publishers to offer trials. The trial stops automatically—no strings attached. Contrary to freeware, which consists of very basic features of software without a time lock, readers are used to receiving full functionality (the entire paper is printed and delivered, and full digital access is provided) *with* a time lock. In a country of seven million households, we estimate that well over a million newspaper trial subscriptions were sold yearly, resulting in a national merry-go-round of customers starting and stopping trial subscriptions. The madness increased when online affiliates entered the game and put all the newspaper trials next to each other on their websites. They made it very easy to get another trial every month.

This hunt for trial users led to a race to the bottom because trial subscribers are very price elastic. The lower the price, the more potential leads you will gather. So if acquisition is down, just drop the price, right? In the Netherlands, it has been common practice to drop the acquisition price of trials to the bare minimum counted by the audit bureau standards as 'paid copies'.

The rise of free apps on mobile phones and thirty-day free trials of services like Netflix has accelerated the race to the bottom in the news industry, because when 'FREE!' enters the game, humans overreact.[18] When choosing between two products, the free product will always win by a landslide, no matter how good the deal or the quality of the other product. And this poses a problem for publishers because marketers are great at copying. Once every competitor

---

18   Dan Ariely, *Predictably Irrational* (New York: HarperCollins, 2008).

in the field has a free thirty-day trial, where do you go next with customers conditioned to getting stuff for free? Sixty days? Ninety days? You may end up devaluing your product and destroying your own market.

The other problem of this strategy is that it attracts the wrong customers. If you attract people who do not benefit from the relationship, the acquisition money is wasted, and the customer will not feel fulfilled.

LOOK FOR VALUABLE CUSTOMERS FROM THE START

We think businesses should do two things to check whether trial subscriptions are the right thing to offer. First, calculate the real margin these trials are generating after deducting taxes, acquisition costs, and variable costs. Don't forget the cost of those calls that did not score a conversion, the prior direct mailings, and all the time invested by the team. Taking all these costs into account, do the trials make money in the long term?

Second, calculate the drop-off of these trials. How many relationships are intact after twenty-four months? After forty-eight months? This requires some proper data preparation because most operational systems cannot follow a customer through time and instead show total amounts of product types. To gain real insights, it is important to track the history of individual customers.

The deeper issue lies with the focus of salespeople and marketers. A typical sales process is like a very wide funnel. At the top are people barely aware of the product or service. The funnel narrows a bit, moving to those who have had some kind of engagement: They visited an event, registered for an e-mail newsletter, saw an advertisement, or heard about the product from friends or coworkers. They may have a latent need for what is on offer. This smaller group has an incentive to investigate further and look at features and price. If they buy the product or service, we are left with a very narrow group compared to the wide top of the funnel. An even lower number of those become loyal relationships.

Wide funnels involve a lot of waste. Many people who interact with your brand will never start a relationship. They may start a new subscription out of optimism, thinking that a subscription to a gym will ensure a weekly workout. Many of them may cancel and feel bad about the decision afterwards. This can lead to bad word of mouth and a negative impact on the brand. Nonetheless, it is common practice amongst marketers to focus on the top of the funnel, using ad campaigns, sampling, and free trials. Some marketers may feel pressured by board members to 'show what we are doing here'. That is why some marketers choose to advertise on billboards along the road that the boss takes to work.

We propose to focus on the bottom of the funnel and then work backwards. Start by looking at the data of core relationships that were acquired a few years back—say, two to five years. Then slice and dice them. Compare trials to regular subscription acquisition. Product A versus Product B. Brand X versus Brand Y. Autopay versus invoice. Telemarketing versus online shop versus retail. Salesperson to individual salesperson.

The lines in your graph that show high drop-off are the channels, brands, offerings, and salespeople to reconsider. No matter how high the initial volume, they are attracting customers who are not interested in the product. At the top of your graph are the products and salespeople with the highest retention. Focus on those channels and offerings for building actual relationships.

In the case of the iPad subscription, we discovered that it was actually the two-year subscription period causing the better retention. New customers got used to the newspaper—it acquired a place in their daily lives. Reading a newspaper can become a strong and valued habit in two years. Then there was the monthly automatic payment. We were so used to quarterly and yearly payment—95 per cent of active subscribers were on these long payment periods—that it never occurred to us that customers prefer drip payment plans. No matter how affluent, people do not like a big bill. The iPad subscription happened to have a monthly payment. Through data, we were able to listen to our customers' needs, and we could establish a relationship.

AN INTELLIGENT THRESHOLD

The trick is to recreate the circumstances that build relationships right at the start of the customer journey. Robbie Baxter calls this a *chute*.[19] When the right prospects are attracted, the sales funnel is a straight line from acquisition to loyalty, without any drop-off. Although this may be an exaggeration (sales will always show some form of a funnel effect), it is important to make the funnel narrower at the top by looking for customers who are prepared to go beyond a trial. We have found success by setting an intelligent threshold for acquisition: one that is high enough to stop low-value customers from entering the business but low enough to let valuable customers in.

---

19   Robbie Baxter, *The Membership Economy* (McGraw-Hill Education, 2015).

How do you know what the right threshold is? We have seen that listening (through data) is one part. The data hinted at the benefits of longer offer periods and monthly payments. The other part was to start an experiment. Our experiment was to offer subscriptions that had monthly payments of an introductory rate that remained in place throughout the term of the offer. A customer would commit to monthly payments for a period of time, and NRC agreed not to increase the price until that term had ended.

The test began with just a small group of sales agents in one particular channel: street sales. Although they were used to selling half-year and year-long subscriptions, we added the two-year option. The agents were very sceptical. 'Nobody wants a longer subscription. It is already very hard to sell an annual offer', they said. It took some convincing. We told them the two-year option could work as a price anchor.[20]

We are all familiar with anchoring: Coffee shops offer small, medium, and large. Most people choose medium. But if there were no large, most people would choose a small coffee, considering medium to be too big. That is how an anchor works. To the surprise of the agents doing the experiment, new customers loved the two-year option; they didn't choose the medium option but went for the large. Not only did the number of annual subscriptions go up but the two-year offer quickly became the most-sold subscription term. So we introduced a new 'large': a three-year term. Today, 56 per cent of all subscriptions sold are three-year. We discovered a new KPI that was much better at predicting relationships than the

---

20   Dan Ariely, *Predictably Irrational.*

number of acquisitions sold. We called it *contract years*, representing the subscription volume that was sold.

After this experiment, we added more street teams to the group selling these new, multiyear offers. We then dropped the half-year contracts, thus drastically increasing the number of years sold per acquisition. While increasing the number of new clients with longer contracts, we stopped selling all automatically stopping trial subscriptions. Those trials were great at the top of the funnel, but they were bad for long-term customer relationships. We could boast about big numbers; we were doing a great job of finding new customers. But the data proved we were not finding the *right* customers.

LONGER SUBSCRIPTION TERMS BUILD STRONGER RELATIONSHIPS

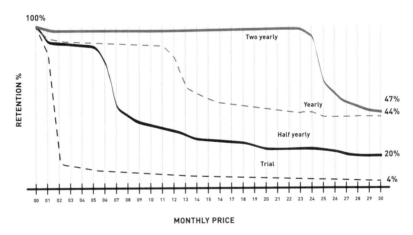

Longer subscription terms build stronger relationships.

When we looked at the actual cost and revenue of the trials, we were shocked to find that the trials had a negative value after deducting all costs, including acquisition and variable costs.

In our case, we also offered a bad customer experience because we did not offer a stripped-down version of our product. We offered the exact same product on trial as on subscription—sometimes for free. And after the trial, we asked people to pay for the same product. In pricing, we call the first price a customer is offered the *reference price* that they will use to gauge the value of the product. A cheap or free trial makes them think of the product or service as inexpensive and perhaps low quality.[21]

As we drifted further from the trial offers, we made a radical decision. We introduced longer contracts in all sales channels. This also took a lot of convincing, but the data was very helpful. We had proof that we had nailed it. It was now time to scale it. Everybody's greatest fear was that we would sell less rather than more, but by the next year, we had increased the number of acquisitions of core subscriptions by 20 per cent. The contract volume went up 130 per cent, even though we were in a highly competitive subscription market that had been going down for almost two decades.

The biggest win was actually something else. We were seeing fewer stops because we had stopped playing the hunting game and subscribers stayed longer. Instead of starting trials over and over again, we started forming relationships. Gone were the many (and expensive) starts of newspaper delivery with a costly follow-up in conversion.

By introducing a threshold of a one-year minimum subscription period, we acquired the right customers: those who have the

---

21   T. Wang, L. Oh, K. Wang et al., "User adoption and purchasing intention after free trial: an empirical study of mobile newspapers," *Information Systems and e-Business Management* 11 (2012).

potential to become relationships. Sometimes it is better to let other customers go if they do not pass the threshold.

NUMBER OF STOPS (NRC)

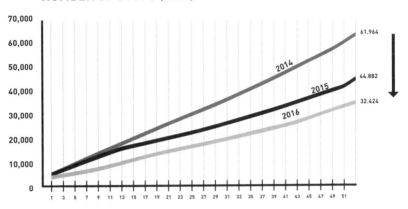

The big win is a huge decrease in stops.

8. UNDERSTAND EMPLOYEES AND THEIR IMPACT ON RELATIONSHIPS

At Mather Economics, one of our clients mentioned in a meeting that he had made a striking discovery. 'Our call-centre representatives generate more revenue each year than we receive from all of our digital advertising.' But guess which activity received more investment in new technologies and data tools? The call centre was underappreciated and underanalysed.

When we examined the performance of the call centre, the project team discovered that the best representatives generated hundreds of thousands of dollars of revenue more than the worst-performing representatives. What caused the differences? What could be done to improve the overall performance? We would learn that the quality of employees defines the quality of the business.

—Matt Lindsay

EMPLOYEES ARE THE BIGGEST ASSET OF EVERY COMPANY

A company is embodied by its employees. They are the face, the voice, and the body of the brand. They see the customers, speak to them, and even touch them. Employees determine how a customer feels and whether a potential customer wants to do business with a company.

Besides the crucial role of representing the company and its brand, it's also true that, despite all of the digital transformations that have taken place, personal sales interactions are still very important for bringing in new customers and negotiating new conditions with existing customers. At NRC, about 70 per cent of the total influx and changes in service are realised by personal sales.

PEOPLE ARE NOT AVERAGE

A lot of companies look at the performance of employees in terms of groups. There is a customer-service group, a call-centre sales group, a group of sales representatives from a particular affiliate company, and many other aggregated groups. They all bring in a number of new clients for a certain cost and are evaluated by those numbers. But if you are interested in optimising sales performance, analysing group averages won't help you. Indeed, they will mislead you and put you on the wrong track because people differ. They are not average, and their performance isn't, either. Some of them are very senior and very good at their job, others are still learning, and some are just not made for sales.

At NRC, we made this mistake with group averages. We regularly analysed the performance of our face-to-face sales teams, who sell subscriptions to passersby in high-traffic shopping locations such as city centres and malls. These teams had a good average ROI (Return On Investment), and that's why we were quite satisfied with their performance—until we got the idea to dig deeper and collected and loaded individual sales data into the data warehouse. This brought us insights on the numbers of each individual agent. It turned out that 80 per cent of the sales were made by 26 people out of the 560 who represented us. The outstanding performance of only 5 per cent of the sales representatives compensated for the miserable results of the other 95 per cent.

Obviously, we were shocked. And we never would have explored this if we had not collected granular data and looked at the individual representatives' performance.

When we discovered these striking results, we realised we had to go 'full monty' in the analysis of the agents. Because we are interested in building long-term relationships, we started to analyse how representatives were performing from a long-term perspective. We looked at the retention of the new customers brought in by the individual agents. This led to a couple of other profound insights.

The data showed that there were sales reps who brought in subscriptions, but over 50 per cent of those were cancelled in the next week. There were also employees who almost never had cancellations. What was happening to cause such divergent results? What were these sales reps doing right and wrong? And who exactly were those people representing our company, day in and day out?

PERFORMANCE SALES REPS (NRC)

(Each bubble is a sales rep, the size of the bubble represents the number of shifts he or she worked)

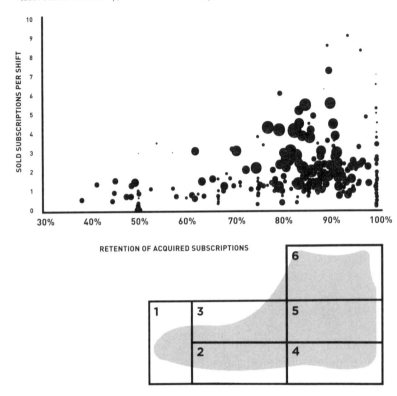

Niels Hoedjes, senior data analyst at NRC, developed 'The Shoe' to analyse sales reps. Each bubble represents a sales rep. On the y-axis is the average number of sold subscriptions per sales shift; on the x-axis is the retention of the acquired customers. The size of the bubble represents the total number of sold subscriptions. Sales reps can be divided in six buckets, ranging from bucket number six, with high sales numbers and high retention, to bucket number one, with low sales and poor retention.

UNDERSTANDING EMPLOYEE EXPERIENCE

To be able to intervene in the sales process in a relevant way, it's crucial to understand who these sales reps are, how they experience their work, and what drives them. That's why we started a project to research the needs and drivers of our internal and external employees involved in sales, using the service-design procedure described in the toolbox in section 5.

We discovered that there were essentially two types of salespeople: those who liked to convince others and those who liked to help new customers find the right product. We analysed their strengths and weaknesses and provided coaching material for each salesperson type, thus increasing their performance and motivation.

We also learned that self-confidence was most important for success in selling a lot of subscriptions. The salespeople had to sparkle. However, this self-confidence was more dependent on what happened during the day than on the personality. A bad remark by a single passerby could drain the energy out of any salesperson. So we started to coach them on how to overcome these bad moments and not let their performance be ruined for the day.

When approached by sales representatives, customers would often check their mobile phone to compare the online price to the one the sales reps were offering. Our sales reps complained that the online price was better. We had heard this point before, but only when we used the service-design procedure described in section 5 did we start to empathise. Before that exercise, we used to think these were just salespeople trying to find an excuse for poor results. Now we feel their pain when customers check the online shop and turn around, saying they will buy the subscription online. So we changed the acquisition pricing in the online shop so that these customers would see that they got a better deal on the spot, with that sales representative. Having a better price than the online sub-scription shop boosts their self-confidence.

IMPROVE SALES RESULTS

We used our data and research insights to optimise sales with some relatively simple adjustments. Often, salespeople are results oriented, so they are driven to reach their KPIs. In some cases, KPIs define their rewards. Again, it's crucial to set the right KPIs to get people running in the right direction.

In our case, we adjusted sales KPIs to stimulate long-term relationships. Originally, that was not the case. There was only one KPI for a sales rep: the number of sold subscriptions. That metric seemed logical but wasn't, because for the salesperson, it didn't matter if the subscriber was still a subscriber after a year. As a matter of fact, it even helped if the subscriber cancelled, because then there would be a hot lead back on the street. So what we did was change the KPI from 'number of subscriptions sold' to 'number of subscription *years* sold.' Sales rewards became solely dependent on the total length of the sold subscriptions. So from then on, one three-year subscription would be worth more than two one-year subscriptions. And when a subscription was cancelled in the first thirty days, there was no reward at all.

Again, this subtle change of the KPI made a big difference for our daily business. The sales managers started to organise sales games to boost the number of subscription years, and the average length of sold subscriptions more than doubled in just one year, from 0.8 to 1.8 subscription years.

CASE STUDY

ANALYSING CALL-CENTRE REPRESENTATIVES' OUTPUT SAVED $1.3 MILLION PER MONTH

OBJECTIVE: A large US cable operator had an inbound call centre that fielded customer-complaint calls and questions from customers regarding rate increases and service fees. The company wanted to weed out bad reps and improve customer experience.

APPROACH: Mather Economics completed an analysis of customer representative performance, showing how effective each rep was at resolving customer issues while saving revenue.

RESULTS: The client used the insights to adjust staffing and training in the call centre. The immediate effect was an incremental revenue gain of $1.3 million per month. Interestingly, the client found that newer customer-service representatives performed better than longer-tenured representatives. They determined that newer reps believed that the current pricing was 'normal,' whereas older representatives were more likely to place customers on lower prices.

REMEMBER

- Pricing has huge impact on financials and relationships.
- Don't let the gut define prices (it never beats data).

- If it's about pricing, analyse real behaviour.

- Forget group averages; understand individual performance.

- Learn what emotionally drives and what burdens salespeople.

- Build intelligent thresholds to acquire customers who want to invest in the long term.

SECTION 3.

SUSTAIN RELATIONSHIPS BY IMPROVING CUSTOMER EXPERIENCE

We found that data analysis is not the only important field of expertise in the Relationship Economy. Listening to real people is just as essential because human emotions don't show up in weekly reports or analyses. This section explains how you can put yourself in your customer's shoes and make better decisions, how you can get organisational silos to cooperate, how you can get leadership support by focusing on customers, and how you can keep your relationships going by giving them ongoing attention.

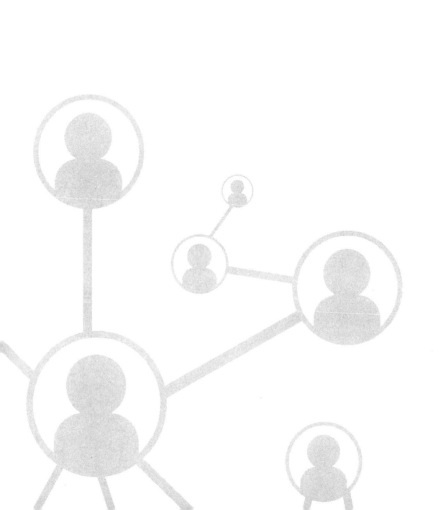

9. SIT DOWN AT THE KITCHEN TABLE

When I pressed the doorbell of the apartment of one of our customers, I felt tired. My workday had been really busy, and I had just travelled two hours through rush hour to the city of Rotterdam to do this interview after work. I would probably not be home before midnight. But my mood changed when I entered the apartment, which was filled with works of fine art and designer furniture. The views overlooking the River Maas were fantastic. My host, one of our readers, was most welcoming, inviting me for a drink at his table while we talked about what role our newspaper played in his life. He loved the content but was very critical about the communication. After twenty-five years, why had we never contacted him before?

He showed me the only thing he received from us: a yearly invoice. It stated the amount to be paid and nothing more. And that amount was quite strange: it ended in cents (our subscription fees are in round euros) and the amount changed every year—sometimes higher, sometimes lower.

'Is that because I had a vacation stop?' he asked. 'Do you subtract those days from my invoice, or do I receive more papers later on?' I looked at the invoice and didn't have a clue. He went on. 'Because of these vague prices, I decided to visit your website to check what the right amount was, only to find out that you are offering lower rates to new customers. That totally enraged me. If you had not visited me this evening, I would probably have stopped the subscription.' Although the invoice turned out to be technically correct, we were losing customers here without realising it.

It may have felt like extra work before I entered the home of this subscriber, but I am really glad I met him personally. We touch base regularly now, and he keeps showing me where we are doing the right or wrong thing. In the ivory tower of the office, we are all too often unaware of what customers are experiencing in the field.

—Xavier van Leeuwe

DATA IS ONLY HALF THE STORY

The road to that customer's apartment really started at a conference where David Kelley of Stanford University explained how he had built a course for noncreative businessmen to become creative and design better experiences for their customers.[22] This is the man who designed the first mouse for Apple. His breakthrough ideas have transformed business, government, and healthcare. And what did it take? Empathy.

We experienced that listening to real people complements listening through data. Through the data, we would never have discovered that a technically correct—yet confusing for customers—invoice could lead to an end of the relationship. When we combined the efforts of data analysis with building empathy for customers, we developed better insights in how to adjust business processes to strengthen those relationships.

FEELING THE NEEDS OF YOUR CUSTOMERS

When we determined that building relationships was the main purpose of our work, it didn't take long before improving customer experience became a top priority. We started with improving some basics, like sending a confirmation e-mail when a customer filled out a complaint form at the website and simplifying the flow of creating a

---

22   Tom and David Kelley, *Creative Confidence: Unleashing the Creative Potential within Us All* (New York: Crown Business, 2013).

digital account.[23] These simple things had never received any attention before because the experience of our loyal customers was not really our concern—we were always too busy acquiring new customers.

The tangible improvements resulted in an immediate drop in customer-service calls, a more top-of-mind position for the subject of customer experience in the company mind-set, and a wish to better understand the feelings of our clients. What do they expect from us? What role does NRC play in their lives? What frustrates them? What do they cherish?

With the help of the Rotterdam-based company Livework, we discovered a method to explore these kinds of feelings: the area of *service design*. Section 5 deals with customer-experience tools and contains a step-by-step explanation of how to understand the deeper needs of your customers.

Building empathy for customers starts with being needs focused, with going beyond studying behaviour, and starting to understand the beliefs and attitudes driving that behaviour. You could call this the part of the iceberg that is underwater. Sometimes, customers have hidden needs that aren't met. It is all about stepping into the mind of your customer. If you are reading their diaries, visiting their house, and sitting at their kitchen table, they will share all their positive and negative feelings about your product and service.

We experienced that when you have placed yourself in the shoes of your customers, they crawl under your skin. You can't forget them once you are back behind your desk. They seem to speak to you from time to time when you are making decisions that

---

23   Other examples of improving customer experience are described in more detail in chapter 10.

will affect the daily lives of customers. That is why we recommend that these interviews take place regularly and be conducted by customer-facing agents, marketeers, board members, and everyone in between. Whether you're from finance, sales, service, production, or accounting, we can all learn from our customers. When more employees have truly empathised with customers, more employees will take that experience back to their daily work, and the company culture will start to change.

BREAKING DOWN SILOS WITH CUSTOMER EXPERIENCE

Getting customer experience on the agenda can do a lot of different things for your company. First of all, it improves relationships with clients, but besides that direct effect, it can also help you to get silos aligned. Customer experience is not a department or a function title. It's more like a shared belief, and most of your coworkers will be open to doing things for customers because in the end, the customers are paying for your daily bread. For that reason, customer experience has the power to break down silos. You can invite everybody in the company to join a project and share their knowledge on customers.

OVERCOME RESISTANCE

There is also a hidden downside to the power of customer experience. Because it's nobody's primary responsibility, there can be resistance to taking on the subject. We experienced three kinds of resistance:

- We are all busy without the extra work.

- It's perceived as touchy-feely and costly.

- Experts prefer to listen to their inner voice.

What can you do to overcome these forms of resistance?

MANAGEMENT SHOULD BE PERSONALLY INVOLVED

The difficulty with tasking everyone to improve customer experience is that it's something else on top of his or her regular work. Nobody is against good experiences for customers, but employees will protest against more work added to their already full agendas. Overcoming this problem starts with the leadership. Middle management makes or breaks the success of a change in culture towards customer centricity. They have to believe in it, put the subject on the agenda, and be personally involved in getting to know the customers. Because when managers don't invest time in customers, why should other employees?

MAKE THE SUBJECT AS HARD AS STEEL

While trying to overcome the resistance to the extra workload of customer experience, it is possible to immediately walk into another form of resistance. Customer experience appears soft—a touchy-feely subject about emotions. From that point of view, it's often disregarded by top managers. Why should you invest any money and time in cuddling? We have a customer-service department, right?

One solution can be to make the project measurable, so you can show its impact in numbers. For example, you could introduce KPIs like a Net Promoter Score.[24] Sometimes it's even possible to make a business case as hard as steel, like we did with our welcome programme.

To improve the experience of new customers, we started a pilot programme in which we called every new subscriber and tried to engage them with our digital products while also checking if delivery of the newspaper was going as planned and if they were happy with the product they chose. We knew this project had to result in a 2.6 per cent decline in cancellations of new subscriptions to earn back the cost of the calls. The pilot resulted in a 3.8 per cent decline in cancellations, which meant the business case was positive: if we implemented this as a standard operating procedure, we would have 1,500 more relationships, a gain of 50,000 euros on the bottom line, and improved customer experience, all at the same time. These kinds of hard numbers help to get trust and support at every level in the organisation.

---

24   The Net Promoter Score (NPS) is a customer-loyalty metric between a provider and a consumer. NPS is calculated based on responses to a single question: How likely is it that you would recommend our company/product to a friend or colleague? The scoring is based on a 0 to 10 scale. The NPS is calculated by subtracting the percentage of detractors (score 0 to 6) from the percentage of promoters (score 9 or 10).

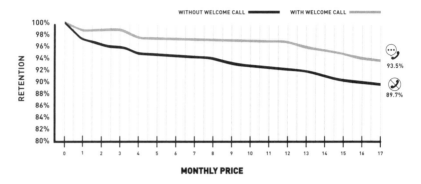

RETENTION NEW SUBSCRIBERS (NRC)

The difference in retention of new subscribers with and without a welcome call. The extra 3.8 per cent retention makes a positive business case and translates to an extra 1,500 relationships a year.

TRAIN YOURSELF AND YOUR COLLEAGUES IN ACTIVE LISTENING

Listening to customers may encounter resistance from experts, especially when they see themselves as responsible for enlightening and surprising customers. Experts tend to strongly believe that innovation is created by brilliant individuals who ignore customer input and rely on their prophetic vision for a better future.

There are two famous quotes that are used often to illustrate why it's not smart to listen to customers. Henry Ford once said, 'If I had asked people what they wanted, they would have said faster horses.' Steve Jobs stated that no customers realised they wanted the iPhone before they saw one. Both quotes basically say that most people don't know about technical innovations and can't tell what a future product should look like. And that's absolutely true.

Customers are not technical experts; that's why customer experience research is not about the specific features of a product.

Customers do, however, know what they need in their lives and what they expect from companies, provided you ask in the right way. Henry Ford probably knew from his customers that they would love fast, reliable, and comfortable transport, and Steve Jobs knew his customers wanted to have the Internet in their pocket. This is also illustrated by a lesser-known quote from Steve Jobs: 'Get closer than ever to your customers. So close that you tell them what they need well before they realise it themselves.'

So how do you get creative, highly specialised, and brilliant individuals interested in connecting to customers? This can be a really hard process because people are who they are, and changing anyone's way of working and thinking is very tough. But it is possible. We taught the skills of listening and understanding the needs of somebody else by following an empathy course and practising active listening in the framework of Thomas Gordon.[25] We trained ourselves to figure out what somebody else really feels, deep inside. This training helped us to interview customers about their needs and to empathise with them. We enriched our inner voice with the voice of the customer.

Techniques for active listening are described in section 5. We also included a tool we created called the *needs matrix*. It incorporates active listening to solve complex business issues with the inclusion of every stakeholder.

---

25   Thomas Gordon, *Leader Effectiveness Training* (New York: The Berkley Publishing Group, 1977).

CASE STUDY

HOW RABOBANK INVESTED IN THE START
OF THE CUSTOMER RELATIONSHIP

By Livework Studio Rotterdam, with Erik Roscam Abbing, Nick Poldermans, and Marit Coehoorn

OBJECTIVE: Understand Rabobank's start-up customers

Rabobank is an international financial-service provider operating on the basis of cooperative principles. One of their marketing managers struggled with pinpointing the challenges, needs, and wishes of customers in the start-up market. Rabobank's market share in this specific market was under pressure. Additionally, new business clients often don't generate revenue over the first couple of years; there is little short-term profit. Therefore, the importance of this group of customers was overlooked.

APPROACH: Getting to know them

The project lasted over a period of four months and consisted of two phases. The 'understand' phase revolved around extensive qualitative research with both current and potential customers. The 'focus' phase revolved around creating new service concepts and building internal understanding. After diving into all existing research on these customers, we recruited sixteen people with different demographics and from separate industries who had recently started a business or were planning to.

Although these conversations had been somewhat prepared and scripted, they were highly explorative, open-ended, and informal. We took great care in ensuring that each interviewee felt comfortable sharing deep emotions and personal stories such as their failures, fears, and frustrations. For instance, people referred to their struggles with making the life-changing decision to start a business. They explained how they coped with the uncertainties and pitfalls of setting up a business and discussed their dreams for the future.

Presentations, business cases, and videos of these entrepreneurs turned out to be essential internal communication that gained commitment from the internal stakeholders at Rabobank. The findings resulted in four profiles of start-up entrepreneurs. The marketing team could use the different profiles and their characteristics to define projects to improve the approach of these customer groups. They presented these projects to their managers including a pitch, a road map, and a business case. Ten top managers joined for a final presentation in which the insights were presented and the proposed projects were pitched.

RESULTS: Totally new marketing strategy

These insights became the basis for all new projects in Rabobank for the start-up market and have been shared with almost all managers at local banks in the business sector. The Rabobank marketing manager reached 120 managers with live presentations and handouts. The project outcomes also resulted in a marketing strategy and campaigns that combined service design with marketing. We called this *marketing as a service*. New product and service ideas are still implemented on a continuous basis. The impact grows continuously, and customers experience this first-hand.

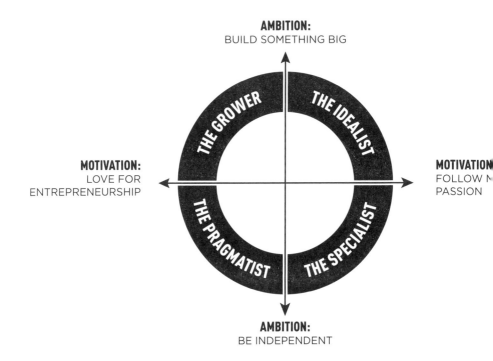

Employing service design: Rabobank found four profiles of start-up entrepreneurs.

10. KEEP INVESTING IN RELATIONSHIPS

When you get into a relationship with a special someone, you may not be equal when it comes to the money side of things. For example, when I met my wife, she already had a serious job and brought in a grown-up salary. On the other hand, I was still in university and was eating beans and tomato sauce at the end of the month. We really liked each other, things were getting serious, and we went out a lot. And she paid, most of the time.

The one thing you don't want is your financial situation messing up the equality in your relationship. To prevent this from happening, I gave small gifts once in awhile to surprise my wife and show her my affection. It didn't take too much effort or money, but it paid off big time—we are still together.

—Matthijs van de Peppel

THE CATCH-22 IN SUBSCRIPTION BUSINESSES

In the relationships between a company and its customers, things are not really different. Customers want and deserve appreciation, especially when you are in a business with recurring fees. Many subscribers read the newspaper for twenty, thirty, or forty years, paying hundreds of euros, and they never hear anything. They don't get a discount or a present, and at the same time there are huge promotions to acquire new subscribers. This frustrates them and they feel cheated. And you know what? They are absolutely right.

However, if we wanted to reward all these loyal customers with, say, a mere 50 euros discount, it could instantly bankrupt the company. And that discount wouldn't even be satisfying for those customers if it wasn't as large as the discount for new subscribers. At the same time, we need those discounts to get new customers to sign up because in the future, they will be the ones paying full price and keeping the business going. From price-elasticity analysis and testing, we know that the influx of new subscribers will dramatically decrease if we stop giving discounts. It feels like a catch-22. There is no solution, because you need the money from your relationships, and you don't have the money to give anything back.

HOW TO INVEST IN CURRENT RELATIONSHIPS WITHOUT GOING BANKRUPT

This sounds like the situation between me and my wife in our dating period, doesn't it? NRC realised the same thing, and we started to think about ways to give little presents to our subscribers.

We did a lot of qualitative research in d.school sessions (explained in detail in section 5). It turned out that our subscribers were not necessarily looking for a discount. Most of them are quite wealthy and don't really care about that. It was about showing attention and gratitude for their business, and money is never the best way to show gratitude. If I had given my wife ten euros once in awhile instead of flowers, I doubt she would be my wife today. Subscribers told us that they just wanted sincere attention, and if we gave a present, it had to do with the newspaper.

The first thing we did was just start to say 'thank you' every once in awhile. We developed an automated e-mail campaign that sends a message from our editor-in-chief on subscription anniversaries. So once in awhile, readers receive an e-mail—just a short message to thank them for their trust in our company, sometimes with a free NRC e-book attached.

What we also did, in cooperation with the head of the service department, was empower our customer-service agents to send personal, handwritten notes to customers. We sometimes sent these to people who had a problem with the newspaper itself, like a delivery issue. But we also sent them to subscribers who faced challenges in their personal life (like stopping the newspaper because they lost their job).

These things are quite simple. They don't require big investments of money or time, but they do make a huge difference for our relationships. For the first time in history, our department started to receive fan mail from subscribers—letters with phrases like, 'Thanks you so much for the get well card. It's so sweet of you to send me this. Amazing service!'

When you take it one step further, you really start investing in relationships and implementing services which cost you money but build relationships. That's what we did with the holiday service: We got rid of the administrative fee to pause the delivery, made sure that customers are able to keep their digital access when they are on holiday (even if they aren't paying at that moment), and started to promote the pause service in the newspaper. The number of holiday breaks increased by 23 per cent, which meant less revenue and less audit bureau circulation for the company. But this is what it takes to build long-term relationships.

WHEN THESE INVESTMENTS PAY OFF

All these things will help to improve customer satisfaction and decrease churn. However, there are two other things that are more important than delighting your customers:

1. **A good product.** When your product is bad, your customers won't be happy, whatever you do in communication or service.

2. **The brilliant basics.** Don't start with fancy stuff if the basics are not brilliant yet. If delivery is failing, fix that before you start sending postcards.

If your product is good and the basics are settled, delighting customers with excellent service, sincere attention, and little gifts will result in an improvement in satisfaction metrics, like the Net Promoter Score. On top of that, it pays off in terms of revenue and number of relationships by decreasing churn. At NRC, churn rates decreased to an all-time low for customers of all ages and in all tenure segments.

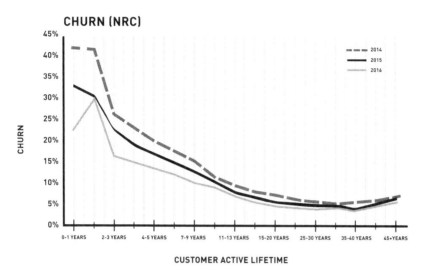

CHURN (NRC)

Improving customer experiences lowered churn in every tenure cohort at NRC.

CASE STUDY

RELATIONSHIP THERAPY FOR THE MASSES

OBJECTIVE: Revive a relationship under strain without suffering huge costs.

APPROACH: Mather Economics and Newsday researched the effects of different affordable gifts on churn prevention. The test was run on subscribers with the highest propensity for stopping, as identified by the prediction model Mather Economics had built. We measured the effects of three kinds of presents on the relationship: a portable smart device charger, a ten-dollar gift card, and a thank-you greeting card.

RESULTS: The greeting card had the greatest short-term effect in retention with the quickest decline in effectiveness, while the charger and the ten-dollar gift card had more permanent effects on retention. Calculating the cost of the incentives and further segmentation of the audience, an optimal strategy for each customer group was found. In a follow-up test, the surprise-and-delight retention-marketing campaigns were tested on subscribers whose churn risk increased from one month to the next. In these cases, the reduction in churn was much greater than the effect on high-churn customers who did not show increasing churn risk. As always in marketing, it is all about timing. It pays to react when the increased churn risk occurs.

SURPRISE AND DELIGHT RETENTION MARKETING FORMERS: TEXT VS. CONTROL

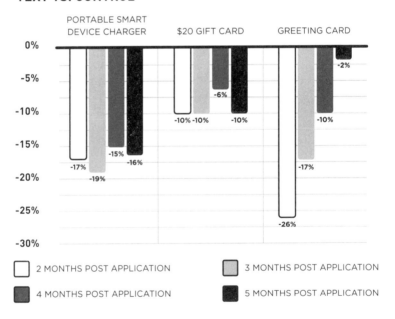

This chart shows the reduction in stopped accounts from targeted accounts in the three retention programs tested at this company.

REMEMBER

- Listening to real people complements listening through data.

- Feeling deeper needs of customers will lead to better decisions and stronger relationships.

- Once you've been in the shoes of your customer, you can't go back.

- Belief in customer experience has the power to break down silos.

- Management has to be personally involved in customer-experience projects.

- Customer experience is not soft; it can increase EBITDA and number of relationships.

- Always keep investing in relationships.

- Maintaining relationships doesn't have to cost a lot of money.

- Track the performance of the relationship-investment initiatives so you can evaluate performance and ROI.

- Brilliant basics and quality of the product come first; special surprises come second.

SECTION 4.

ANALYTICAL TOOLS TO INCREASE THE VALUE OF RELATIONSHIPS

The key to the effective application of analytics to a business is the combining of managerial initiative with analytical insight. Without the decision to conduct business processes differently in light of new information, the insight provided from analytics and big-data investments will yield little.

In this section, we will discuss analytical-modelling techniques that have been 'packaged' with a specific business application in mind to create an analytical tool. Rather than describe the technical modelling approaches employed, we will discuss the context in which they are applied within a business. The analytical tools described in this section can be employed in businesses with or without recurring revenue. The key to success is to start with the application in mind and work backwards to select a modelling approach and the required data.

Customer analytics can predict aggregate behaviour, such as subscribers' likelihood of stopping their service, and there are several modelling approaches that are well suited to this purpose, such as discrete choice models, survival models, and machine-learning techniques. The common ingredient in all of these models is data on past customer activity. In this section, we will go light on the econometric modelling-tool discussion and instead offer guidance on the equally important but often overlooked critical ingredient in successful analytical projects: execution of business strategies using insights from the analysis. Certain best practices and helpful lessons are covered in this section too, including the importance of utilising data at the most helpful level of detail (often called its *granularity*).

11. CUSTOMER LIFETIME VALUE (CLV)

My first job out of graduate school was as an economic analyst for a large package-delivery company. My group studied the marginal costs of adding package volume to the delivery network. The company had a cost model that allocated costs to different customers, and a large portion of the delivery network cost was allocated to a customer based on the number of pieces at their delivery stop. Residential customers typically had only one or two packages per stop, while commercial customers had ten or more. As a result, the allocated cost of residential customers was much higher than commercial customers, and there was serious discussion of eliminating residential deliveries. Before that decision was made, we realised that residential deliveries filled a part of the day (between commercial deliveries early in the day and commercial pick-ups late in the day) when the driver would have little to do otherwise. Thus, the marginal cost of adding residential volume to the business was low. Eliminating these residential delivery stops would not have eliminated much cost while also lowering revenue considerably. A misunderstanding of customer profitability and lifetime value almost caused this company to make an immense mistake.

—*Matt Lindsay*

In our work with companies analysing customers, we find that a powerful metric is CLV. This metric supports many of the tools described later in this section. For instance, you can use CLV to determine the right retention campaign to use for a customer segment by finding the campaign attributes that maximise the return on investment. CLV can also be an important input to determining the right pricing strategy for subscribers, both at the point of acquisition and when they renew their service.

We define CLV as the expected stream of operating margins from a customer over a period of time. For many businesses, it makes sense to define the time horizon to be used for calculating the metric, and we find that companies usually set this horizon at two or three years. In calculating the operating margins by customer, it is important to include only direct costs and revenue, as these variables will change if customers leave or new customers are added. Including allocated fixed costs in the CLV calculation can lead to incorrect customer-profitability measurements, because some customers may appear unprofitable when in fact they take advantage of slack resources or are inexpensive to serve.

CLV also provides valuable intelligence to several operational processes that maintain customer relationships, such as retention call centres and customer-acquisition campaigns. In a retention call centre, customer-service representatives can have different authority levels to 'save' a customer based on their CLV. For acquisition campaigns, the customer characteristics that drive high CLV (such as auto bill pay) can be used for targeting acquisition channels or designing acquisition offers.

When calculating CLV, it is important to use a predicted lifetime for customers instead of static, historical retention curves, because many actions that affect a customer's lifetime value have off-setting effects on parts of the CLV calculation. For example, raising a customer's monthly subscription price will increase revenue per month, which will raise that customer's lifetime value. However, a price increase will also increase the customer's likelihood of stopping service, which will have a negative effect on expected lifetime. The net effect of the price increase on a customer's lifetime value will depend on whether the lost expected lifetime effect on CLV is less than the effect of the higher revenue per month. A CLV model that does not use dynamic predictions of customer lifetime will not be able to accurately predict changes in CLV.

AN EXAMPLE OF A CLV CALCULATION IN THE WIRELESS INDUSTRY

Calculating the CLV of a wireless customer can be done using the following formula:

CLV = [(ARPU – CCU)*Expected Lifetime] – CPGA

ARPU is average revenue per unit, CCU is cash cost per user, and CPGA is cost per gross add (the cost of acquiring a new customer). For existing customers, the acquisition cost will not be included in the calculation. The expected-lifetime calculation is often developed using survival models, a tool we will discuss in chapter 15.

The graphic below identifies the elements that affect CLV for the wireless business. Changes in each variable can have positive or negative effects on the CLV, and the magnitude of the effect can be quantified through the CLV framework.

ATTRIBUTE	BASELINE	CHANGE	EFFECT				
			CLV	CPGA	ARPU	CCU	LIFETIME
Customer Type	New	Existing	↑	↓	↔	↔	↔
Aquisition Month	April	May	↑	↔	↑	↑	↑
		February	↓	↔	↓	↓	↓
Handset Age	12 months	Increase	↓	↔	↓	↓	↓
Income Tier	4	Increase	↑	↔	↑	↑	↑
Age	43	Increase/Decrease	↔	↔	↔	↔	↔
Average MOU	1,486	Increase	↓	↔	↔	↑	↔
Average IVR	12	Increase	↓	↔	↓	↓	↓
Gender	F	M	↑	↔	↑	↑	↑
Unpaid Balances/ Write-offs	$20	Increase	↓	↔	↓	↓	↓
Auto Bill Pay Status	No	Yes	↑	↓	↑	↑	↑
ODP (Handset Revenue)	$100	Increase	↑	↔	↑	↔	↔
Monthly Contract Price	$45	Increase	↑	↔	↑	↔	↔
Monthly Fee Revenue	$10	Increase	↑	↔	↑	↓	↓

As we often say, data by itself is worthless. What you do with the data makes it valuable. A dynamic CLV calculation is a robust analytical approach for making profit-maximising strategic and tactical decisions. The incremental profit created by these decisions should yield a substantial return on the investments in the data and analytics required for CLV projection.

12. CHURN MODEL

'Tell us which customers are about to stop so we can call them', is a request we hear often. We reply that we can tell them how many will stop (and who is the most likely), but not exactly which customers will stop. The power of predictive models employed in customer analytics is typically reflected in aggregate numbers across customer segments. The behaviour of an individual customer is binary; that person will either continue service or not, which means that if there's an estimated 50 per cent chance of stopping, the error rate will be large in either outcome. When we look at a group of one hundred customers who all have a 50 per cent estimated chance of stopping, we can reasonably expect fifty to stop, and our error rate will not be large if we miss by one or two stops either way.

At Mather Economics, we have had several clients that were impressed by the accuracy of customer-churn predictions; however, many were at a loss for what to do with that information. They could not think of opportunities in their current operations to improve their customer retention by lowering stops. Conversely, we have other clients that are very innovative and entrepreneurial in using insights derived from analytics to focus their efforts on the highest-risk customers.

One of these innovative clients coined the phrase 'from one-size to personalise' to describe their philosophy. They had repeated success in moving from a one-size-fits-all approach to a customer-facing, segmented, and focused approach. They changed billing notices from a standard sequence of messages that started at the same point in a subscription lifecycle for all customers to a messaging sequence that started once they identified a deviation from prior behaviours (a key predictor of a customer's likelihood to churn).

Churn models are good at estimating relative probabilities across the customer base, and we can provide a list of the customers with the highest probabilities of closing their account. We have tested alternative retention efforts for several clients to see which worked best at the lowest incremental cost per saved customer. Focusing your retention efforts on the group of customers where the return on investment is greatest will have a tremendous effect on your overall subscription base.

Once you have a churn model, the next step is to identify opportunities to change current processes to leverage this insight. The best implementation opportunities are those where a relatively small improvement in performance can have significant financial benefits. In this book, we discuss call-centre performance and the surprising amount of revenue that those representatives handle on behalf of the company. These reps are fielding calls from customers who contact the company in regards to a bill, service issue, or other question. With churn models, you are able to take proactive steps to mitigate a customer's potential deactivation or service cancellation, but you have to know in advance the target performance improvement that will provide the desired return on investment.

CASE STUDY

PERSONALISING MESSAGES REGARDING PAST-DUE PAYMENTS LOWERS CHURN BY 14 PER CENT

OBJECTIVE: A large US publisher wanted to reduce the percentage of subscribers entering a grace period and ultimately stopping due to nonpayment.

APPROACH: Mather Economics leveraged historical payment data to create profiles at the subscriber level. Normal distribution windows were calculated to measure whether a subscriber had fallen outside of normal payment patterns. The publisher used this data to send dynamic e-mail messages to customers who had not made a payment within their normal window, reminding them to remit payment.

CONDITION: SUB OUTSIDE NORMAL PAYMENT PATTERN (AVG. DAYS + 1 SD)
DYNAMIC MESSAGE #1
John, thank you for being a valued subscriber. We hope you are pleased with your service. For assistance with your account, please call customer service at (555) 555-5555.

CONDITION: SUB OUTSIDE NORMAL PAYMENT PATTERN (AVG. DAYS + 1 SD) AND NO PAYMENT 14 DAYS AFTER MESSAGE #1
DYNAMIC MESSAGE #2
John, this is a reminder that payment is now due. For assistance with payment, please call customer service at (555) 555-5555.

CONDITION: SUB OUTSIDE NORMAL PAYMENT PATTERN (AVG. DAYS + 1 SD) AND NO PAYMENT 14 DAYS AFTER MESSAGE #2
DYNAMIC MESSAGE #3
John, this is a reminder that your payment is now past due. For assistance with payment, please call customer service at (555) 555-5555.

RESULTS: The dynamic messaging test reduced nonpay churn by 14 per cent versus a control group at ninety days postapplication. The significant reduction in churn was achieved through a series of three sequential e-mail messages, where subscribers only received the second message if payment was not received within two weeks of the first message, and so forth. Because the messages were delivered via e-mail, the marginal cost was essentially zero. Testing showed that personalised e-mail messaging tailored to individual payment profiles can have a significant impact on increasing payment rates and reducing churn due to nonpayment.

13. REVENUE AND AUDIENCE-VOLUME FORECAST MODEL

'We are missing our budget because the renewal-pricing changes are not generating the incremental revenue that we expected', audience-revenue managers have been known to say. We find it is most often the case that the revenue forecast in the budget was developed incorrectly and the revenue yield from pricing changes is close to what was initially projected. This is not surprising, as revenue forecasting in a recurring-revenue business is difficult. Besides being an important planning tool that enables a business to evaluate strategic alternatives, a well-developed revenue and volume forecast can provide enormous value in managing a business throughout the year.

The process of maintaining customer relationships using data and analytics described in this book will increase the complexity of the subscription operation, and as a result there will be a growing need for more sophisticated revenue forecasting and budgeting. There are two types of revenue forecasting: top-down and bottom-up. Top-down forecasting typically extrapolates trends in revenue, volumes, and rates to estimate future performance. 'Last year plus two per cent' is a typical example of this type of forecasting. The fundamental problem of this approach is that it is detached from the causal relationships underlying the trends. There is no way to quantify the effect of an increase in churn or a drop in customer starts on total revenue.

We advocate a bottom-up budgeting approach for recurring-revenue businesses. In this approach, the forecasting process starts with the number of customer acquisitions, estimated cancellations by customer segment, and expected levels for other types of customer activity. Using a bottom-up approach, the cumulative effect of all customer activity will determine the revenue forecast and the effect of deviations from the planned activity levels or average revenues per customer will be evident in the top-line numbers.

As we mentioned, differences in any type of customer activity that would affect the budget will be reflected in the revenue forecast. This is important, as businesses with recurring-customer revenue (such as subscriptions) are subject to the compounding effect over multiple time periods. Small differences from the forecast each week will result in large differences over time. A shortfall of one hundred net customer acquisitions in a week may not be noticeable in the current financial results, but if this shortfall occurs every week, the cumulative effect will be substantial. Identifying problems early and taking corrective action as soon as possible will avoid much larger problems and harder solutions later in the year. That is why we advocate not only a bottom-up approach to budgeting but also a more frequent, often weekly, update of the revenue and volume forecasts.

An interesting observation we've made while revenue forecasting with our subscription clients is the time it takes for a subscription business to reach equilibrium following a change in their operations. If a business makes improvements to their retention campaigns that lower average weekly customer losses by 10 per cent, the number of active customers will grow until the number of weekly stops is once again equal to the weekly starts. For an easy mathematical example, suppose a business has one thousand customers with average retention of 50 per cent per year. This company will have about five hundred stops per year, or about ten per week, so they will need about ten new starts per week to maintain their existing customer volume of one thousand. If they were to cut their weekly stops by 10 per cent, so they lose nine customers a week instead of ten, their customer base will grow by one customer each week if they maintain new starts at their current level.

When will they stop growing? The company will add customers until they once again reach ten stops per week at the new retention rate, which will be around 1,111 customers. Adding those 111 customers will take a little over two years. This considerable adjustment period is emblematic of the challenges facing subscription businesses. Changes to the operating processes take a long time to be completely reflected in a company's performance metrics. Patience is a rare commodity in many businesses—particularly when results are tracked against annual budgets—and it is tempting for management to make further adjustments before the prior changes have reached their natural conclusion.

CASE STUDY

HOME-DELIVERY AUDIENCE REVENUE
AND VOLUME FORECASTING

OBJECTIVE: A US publisher wanted to accurately forecast home-delivery circulation revenue for 2016, with periodic updates based on actual performance.

APPROACH: Mather Economics used historical subscription data to estimate key factors in circulation budgeting, including base-subscriber attrition, start frequency, start retention, price sensitivity, and seasonality. Mather and the client discussed strategic plans for 2016 and how they would differ from past years to strengthen the forecast. After an initial evaluation period, Mather began updating the forecast weekly with actual data.

RESULTS: Through the first five months of 2016, Mather's prediction of total revenue was less than a tenth of a per cent below actual revenue for that time period. The variance was primarily due to higher-than-projected new start prices and fewer stops as a result of pricing. In June 2016, Mather updated projected revenue to reflect the observed trends in pricing and new start revenue. These forecasts were then updated weekly to account for actual performance and help the client identify important trends. By July 2016, projections showed total revenue for 2016 as 2.02 per cent higher than originally projected.

14. COMPREHENSIVE DATA GATHERING WITH LISTENER

One of our clients asked us for assistance in maximising total digital revenue. To understand their current revenue streams, we requested data from their advertising server (usually Google's DFP) and their site traffic, showing how their content was consumed by their online audience. The site traffic data was typically captured by Google Analytics or Adobe's Omniture. What we found was that the data from these two systems was not easily combined at the user level. It was impossible to see, by individual, what users were reading and what advertising revenue they were generating. To bridge this data gap, we developed Listener, a tagging solution that places JavaScript and other code into the applications running on a web page so that data from the ad server, video player, paywall, and content-management system were captured simultaneously.

Listener data is not the only tool for understanding digital-audience economics, but it is a convenient and inexpensive option.

With Listener data, you can develop a set of business rules for content access that maximise the expected digital revenue (both advertising and audience revenue) from a customer. If a site visitor is running an ad blocker, you will see that their advertising revenue is $0, and you can refuse to give them access to content. If the user is reading two hundred articles a month and generating $20 in advertising revenue, you can provide them all the content they will consume. It is possible to model individual users' likelihood of subscribing to the product using the data captured by Listener from prior subscription offers.

CASE STUDY

MAXIMISING TOTAL DIGITAL REVENUE WITH DYNAMIC CONTENT ACCESS

OBJECTIVE: A medium-sized US publisher wanted to grow online subscriber conversions through the paywall while not risking advertising revenue. They wanted to understand how to adjust their metered paywall to maximise net digital revenue.

APPROACH: Mather Economics collected detailed, event-level data from the publisher's website to understand how each user behaved and interacted with the paywall. Advertising revenue per page and user, along with expected probability for each user converting to a paid subscription, were analysed and prepared as an easy-to-use, Excel-based revenue forecasting model. The client, with the support of Mather Economics, was able to input different paywall and advertising assumptions to identify risk/reward. Mather delivered recommendations to adjust the paywall, which were implemented in the paywall system and measured.

RESULTS: Overall, subscriptions through the paywall grew by nearly 15 per cent in the first month, while advertising revenue remained constant. Certain environmental attributes (device, location, time of day, etc.) were found to be important, but even more important were the behaviour, engagement, and content consumed. Through this analysis and application, the publisher now understands the value of their online content and audience from both a subscription and an advertising perspective.

CASE STUDY
USING LISTENER DATA TO ANALYSE AUDIENCE ECONOMICS

OBJECTIVE: A digital publisher in a major US metropolitan market with two Major League Baseball teams had an audience large enough to support a digital sports product as an add-on to their core publication, and they wanted to determine how much content should be offered to each group for free to maximise total digital revenue.

APPROACH: One of the teams had a digital audience that was largely national in its distribution, while the other team's digital audience was almost exclusively local. From an advertising-revenue perspective, that meant that the team with a local audience generated much more traffic that could be sold through the direct sales force to local advertisers at higher rates. The other team had about half of their digital traffic from fans living outside the local metropolitan area, the advertising for which was sold through programmatic channels at a lower rate. The team with the national audience had a higher propensity to subscribe, in part because the out-of-town audience was eager to have access to the coverage that their local sports did not cover in detail.

The national audience also had demographic characteristics that were found to be indicative of subscription buyers. The local team's fans could read the coverage through the print platform or other local coverage, so they had less demand for access to digital coverage. Also, they tended to have attributes indicative of a group less likely to subscribe, such as a younger age profile and a greater share of mobile-content consumption.

RESULT: The CLV calculation using Listener data demonstrated that fans from the team with a more local audience should get more free content than fans from the team with a more national audience. We found that the opportunity cost of lost advertising revenue from a more restrictive access policy to the local audience outweighed the likely additional subscription revenue that would be realised. The opposite was true of the team with the more national audience.

15. YIELD MANAGEMENT FOR RECURRING REVENUE

Subscription and other recurring-revenue businesses have a significant advantage over other companies in the number of times they interact with their customers. They can observe a customer's behaviour over time and adjust the nature of their services to maximise the lifetime value of that relationship. One of the ways they can adjust their relationship with a customer is through the pricing of their product or service, particularly when it is time for that customer to renew his or her service.

When Mather Economics first started working with publishers, we noticed they had a lot of demographic data on their subscribers, but they were not using the data in the audience department. The customer-demographic data was used exclusively to market their audience to their advertising customers. They could show advertisers the demographic profile of their readers, the geographic distribution by ZIP code, and the overlap between their readership and the customers of the advertiser. Publishers were not using this data to understand which of their customers were most likely to cancel after a price increase, to churn for another reason, or to upgrade their subscription.

In 2002, Matt Lindsay had recently left Arthur Andersen Business Consulting following the Enron paper-shredding controversy, and was working as an independent consultant for Knight Ridder, the second-largest newspaper publishing company at the time. They had hired him to analyse their subscription pricing strategy following several years of declining audience volumes and revenue despite aggressive discounting of subscription prices. 'We had a Harvard MBA work on this, but he did not find anything', they told him. 'We do not think you will either, but we are willing to give you a try.'

Knight Ridder sent data from the subscription system at one of their newspapers, the *St. Paul Pioneer Press*, to begin the analysis. When this data was plotted as a retention chart, it was clear that retention behaviour of subscribers was remarkably similar to data Lindsay had seen on patient lifespans in healthcare economics in graduate school. The similarity brought to mind survival analysis as a possible approach for modelling subscriber retention and price elasticity.

Survival analysis is the field of statistics used to analyse patient data, and this same type of econometrics can be used to predict machinery failures and comparable events in other fields. The goal of survival models in healthcare is to understand what factors affect the lifespan of a patient. In applying this analytical approach to the publishing industry, we were interested in predicting how long a particular subscriber would remain active as a customer. The 'failure event' to be predicted in healthcare economics is a patient's death. In models for publishers, it was a cancelled subscription.

Using survival analysis, it was clear that price increases played a role in a subscriber's likelihood of stopping, but the effect of price was very different across different segments of the customer base. Certain groups of customers were twenty times more likely than others to stop after a price increase. It quickly became clear that a one-price model was not the best strategy for publishers. Much like other industries that had been through significant change and disruption, such as airlines and hotels, publishing could use sophisticated pricing analytics to increase revenue and operating margins.

Our first few tests of this insight involved targeted pricing adjustments for groups of subscribers who appeared to be paying much less than they would be willing to pay for the product. It was not uncommon for publishers to have below-optimal subscription prices due to the value incremental subscribers brought to the advertising-revenue stream. Indeed, the first tests showed that some customers showed very little reaction to price increases, while others had significant reactions.

Eventually, we developed a recurring process where subscriber data was sent by our clients every week, and we returned suggested renewal prices for each account. Statistically representative control groups were used to measure the effect of prices on retention and revenue, and the industry gradually accepted that this type of pricing was beneficial for both the customers and the publishers. We now perform this kind of analysis for about five hundred publications in twelve countries on four continents. These clients provide us with subscriber data on about thirty million households every week.

You may wonder how charging different prices for the same product works in a Relationship Economy. It really depends on local customs, and you need to understand what feels right for the organisation and for your customers. Some compare this differentiated pricing to progressive taxation. We do not expect everyone to pay the same amount of tax every year because the tax is determined by income levels and certain life circumstances. Similarly, a $500 per year newspaper subscription is a much greater percentage of disposable income to a schoolteacher, on average, than it is to an investment banker. Arguably, investigative journalism is a public good that benefits everyone once it is produced. Differentiated pricing could be seen as benefiting society as a whole due to greater support for journalism and greater access to independent news.

Many of our big-picture findings about subscriber retention are intuitive. As expected, the more a subscriber's renewal price is increased, the more likely it is that the customer will cancel the subscription. But that fact hides important distinctions between individual subscribers. Price sensitivity varies considerably across a publisher's subscriber base, and our detailed knowledge of the differences can be used to minimise customer cancellations due to a price increase. This type of pricing strategy can reduce cancellations due to a price increase by up to 75 per cent.

As we suspected, customers with higher incomes are less sensitive to price increases than those with lower incomes. At the end of the four years, for the average subscription cohort, there are about twice as many high-income subscribers remaining as low-income subscribers. This result would suggest that income is an important variable to consider in pricing and retention strategies.

A further disaggregation of the retention data to isolate subscribers acquired by one channel (in this case, inserts) shows that the effect of income on retention is much lower within a single acquisition channel. While high-income customers still have higher retention, the variation across income levels is smaller, particularly in the first few years of the customer lifecycle.

If we plot retention across acquisition channels for the high-income group only, we see that there is considerably more variation in retention across channels within the income tiers than we saw across income levels. This insight suggests that the nature of the acquisition offer and method of acquisition play an important role in retention—perhaps more so than income level. These are but two of the factors affecting retention that we include in our survival models. Other variables include subscription term, payment method, seasonal patterns, demographic variables, and macroeconomic indicators.

One advantage of regression modelling (such as survival analysis) is that it is able to measure the effects of each important factor in isolation. Visualisation tools are very helpful in uncovering relationships within the data and presenting results to a broad audience. Complementing regression modelling with A/B testing, performance measurement, and reporting is the best way to establish a closed-loop pricing-and-retention optimisation process where insights from prior price changes are incorporated into future changes, thus improving the efficiency and performance of the pricing strategy.

With digital subscriptions, the number of variables that can be included in survival models increases substantially. A number of predictive metrics are consistently important in our models of retention of digital subscribers. We can classify these metrics into consumption, interaction, attitudinal, time, and socioeconomic categories, although there are other metrics that do not fall into these groups.

Consumption metrics describe the quantity, frequency, and time spent with the content during a particular period of time. *Interaction* metrics describe actions taken by customers while on the site or while they are engaged with the content. *Attitudinal* metrics are those that measure the level of an individual's enthusiasm for or loyalty to a topic or community. *Time* metrics reflect when events occurred during a subscriber's lifecycle and the overall time of activity on the account, often called the *account tenure*. *Socioeconomic* metrics include factors that characterise an individual's demand for the product, such as disposable income, price sensitivity, age, gender, macroeconomic indicators, education, and household type.

Using survival analysis and other types of customer analytics, we have made adjustments to retention strategies, operational processes, and prices. We have found that data-supported actions can reduce churn by 15 per cent in the first few weeks, and the performance usually gets better as publishers learn from their initial efforts. Pricing strategies can reduce price-related customer losses by as much as 75 per cent.

Given the changes to the advertising industry, it is likely that the majority of revenue for publishers will come directly from their audiences. Using data and analytics to manage customer acquisition, retention, and pricing strategies as well as possible will make the difference between the publishers that survive and those that do not.

It is important to note that analytics on customer price elasticity are only the first step in an effective subscription yield-management process. There are necessary technical implementation steps within the billing and customer-relationship management systems, and it is imperative that testing and reporting processes be in place so that the effectiveness of the pricing analytics can be monitored and insights from the pricing changes can be incorporated into future yield-management decisions. An often overlooked but critical element to a successful yield-management programme is a thoughtful strategy for customer communication and messaging of the price changes, including customer-service scripts for responding to questions from subscribers. We have found that messaging and customer communication are very important to the ultimate performance of the programme because they have such a significant effect on the bottom-line yield from the price changes.

The combination of 'hard' analytics with 'soft' customer-relationship management is critical for organisations that seek to manage customer revenue for the long-term health of their business. At Mather Economics, we have helped hundreds of businesses implement the analytics, testing, reporting, and communication elements of a yield-management programme, and we have developed metrics that capture the effectiveness of these two sides of the project. When we work with clients on subscriber-pricing projects, we find that the value we provide often comes from our experience with the communication and messaging of the pricing process to the final customer, which is a critical step in sustaining the customer relationship.

CASE STUDY

**REDUCING PRICE-RELATED CHURN THROUGH
TARGETED SUBSCRIPTION PRICING**

OBJECTIVE: A midsized US publisher needed to increase audience revenue to offset changes in advertising revenue while minimising customer-volume losses.

APPROACH: Mather Economics analysed data on each subscriber to estimate customer sensitivity to price increases and determine the ideal price adjustments upon renewal. Changes in total expected revenue and volume from the price changes were estimated. Recommended price changes by account were provided on a weekly basis along with a representative sample of accounts for a control group. Performance reports were produced weekly to carefully monitor the pricing campaign.

RESULTS: The programme was closely monitored by Mather Economics and the client. By strategically applying varying price increases at the subscriber level, the client realised a circulation revenue increase of 8.7 per cent over a nine-month period while incurring only a 1.38 percentage-point increase in subscriber cancellations. Mather actively examined each segment's performance and adjusted the pricing actions in response to the findings. After a successful initial-pricing round, the publisher is now confident and prepared to move forward with another pricing increase to bolster their financial position in the upcoming fiscal year.

Below is a chart of customer retention for target accounts that received a price change and for control accounts that did not. Stops due to the price change led to the difference in retention between these two groups.

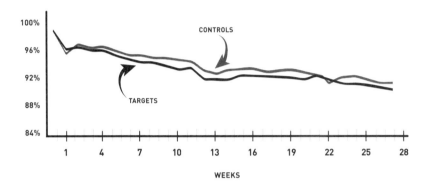

QUESTIONS TO ASK AS YOU BEGIN AN ANALYTICS PROJECT TO GROW REVENUE

Pricing decisions involve not only questions of revenue and volume but also about the overall relationship with customers. Some businesses prefer less price differentiation, and others prefer more, depending on their strategies and market circumstances. These questions have been addressed by many of our customers, and we felt it would be helpful to share them here.

News media is an industry near and dear to our hearts. Often, publishers and CEOs are not familiar with the dynamics of audience revenue because they rose through the editorial or advertising departments. In addition, news-media companies have often been very profitable in the past, so optimising audience revenue was not a priority. The company could rely on advertising revenue, and as a result, publishers often just raised customer prices across the board without big concerns over the lost customer volume. Similarly, editorial teams tend to focus on readership and do not have much experience with audience revenue, retention, and acquisition. Only recently, as the industry has been disrupted by new digital platforms, have the issues of customer revenue and engagement received significant attention.

The following are brief discussions of issues to consider as you develop a pricing strategy for your recurring-customer revenue.

VOLUME OR MARGIN

Companies consider several factors when answering this question, particularly firms that derive other revenue streams from the size of their customer base: advertising for publishers, interest income for banks, or in-app purchases for game developers. Where other revenue streams are significant, having higher customer volume is helpful. It is important to optimise the revenue derived from these revenue streams holistically. On a related note, it is important to include different departments in the pricing-strategy discussion in order to understand the effect of changes to one revenue stream on all other revenue streams.

SLOW AND STEADY OR FULL THROTTLE

If additional revenue is needed quickly, an accelerated test-and-learn process can be implemented. An ideal implementation is to use a small but statistically valid sample of the customer base in a test of possible pricing options, but this will typically require several months to produce meaningful results. Alternatively, several test groups that include a greater number of customers can be implemented simultaneously so insights are derived quickly and revenue is increased sooner rather than later. The risk from this strategy is an adverse reaction from one of the pricing test groups that negates some of the benefits. Also, the degree of pricing changes plays a big part in the risk-and-return calculation in the slow-versus-fast testing decision.

LIGHT TECH OR HIGH TECH

You may be worried that you and your IT group have to invest a lot of time in connecting systems to implement targeted recurring-revenue pricing strategies or to deal with vulnerabilities in your payment-processing or other operational systems. The IT investment is often far less than what most companies expect, but where there are significant IT challenges, a pilot programme can be implemented—again, without committing too many resources.

SIZE AND NATURE OF CONTROL GROUP

Using a control group to evaluate the effect on pricing and retention is an incredibly valuable tool, and we strongly recommend this approach to our customers even after the testing phase is completed. There is an opportunity cost from using a control group: the foregone revenue from not including these customers in the price increase. To minimise the lost revenue, the control group size can be selected as efficiently as possible to obtain a statistically valid sample, and the pricing tests can be designed so that this group also sees an increase of some sort in an across-the-board manner. Although not as accurate as a no-increase control group for measuring price elasticity, this method does provide insights into relative price elasticity across customer segments.

DIFFERENTIATED OR PER PRODUCT

You will get the best results in customers saved (volume) and correct pricing (margin) if you have an individual customer pricing strategy. One customer's rate may go up 20 per cent while another's rate may only increase 2 per cent. However, if you worry about clients having a bad experience or about bad public relations, then you can choose less-granular pricing strategies, such as separate increases per product or per bundle (like NRC did). Once you have an understanding of the variation in price elasticity across your customer base, the trade-off between pricing at the customer, product, region, or other level of granularity can be estimated. In Mather Economics's experience, the benefits of targeted pricing outweigh the costs.

WHAT DATA TO USE IN THE PRICING DECISION

What type of customer data will be included in the analysis of pricing elasticity and the yield-management process? Are any data fields sensitive for you or your customers? Are any practices prohibited by law? Typically gender, race, and religion are excluded from pricing decisions. Other variables can be considered for inclusion or exclusion, such as online consumption, where cookie permission is often needed. Customer tenure is typically a very valuable factor for estimating price elasticity, as is income. Age group can be helpful too. In most cases, demographic data on customers is aggregated to the ZIP + 4 level in the United States and comparable geographic areas in other countries. Additional customer data will make your modelling and revenue strategies more accurate and efficient.

TRADE-OFFS BETWEEN PERSONAL DATA PRIVACY AND CUSTOMER ANALYTICS

A fundamental question has arisen from the ubiquitous capturing of data enabled by digital distribution platforms: Where and when do the costs of data capture outweigh the benefits? There are costs from capturing the data in the form of large websites and slower page-load times, which have been found to alter customer behaviour in ways that lower the revenue of the publisher. There are also costs from capturing data in terms of the loss of privacy a customer experiences from being tracked. What are the benefits and costs of this lost privacy?

One of the most significant differences between European companies and their American counterparts is their sensitivity about using information they collect about their customers. Does the reluctance to use customer data to optimise their businesses hinder European companies? The answer, at least in one respect, seems to be yes.

According to newspaper association WAN-IFRA, in the five years from 2011 to 2015, news-media companies in Europe lost 21.3 per cent of their print circulation, while in the United States the loss was 8.7 per cent.[26] There are several factors that affect these

---

26   WAN-IFRA, "World Press Trends Report 2016."

numbers, including the greater reliance on single-copy sales in Europe, but a significant factor has been the more rapid adoption of customer analytics to segment and target customers for pricing actions, retention efforts, and bundle offers. American companies are rapidly adopting customer analytics to acquire digital subscribers. This use of customer data by publishers has arguably retained millions of newspaper subscribers who would otherwise no longer be customers had US news media adopted European standards of data usage.

The use of consumer data by companies is fundamentally driven by the profit motive, and consumers accept that their personal data will be used by companies to offer them products and services directly or to help other companies advertise to them. This social compact has worked well, providing vast consumer benefits in the form of thousands of products and services available at little or no cost. Excluding breaches of financial data such as credit-card numbers, damages from companies' use of personal data have been difficult to prove in court. However, economists could argue that consumers may be harmed by the reduction in value of their personal information due to the widespread availability of that data, and the lack of legal damages does not mean that there are no costs to consumers from the use of their personal data.

Consumers have learned that some advertising is annoying, that information sharing may lead to more spam e-mail, or that it could make them more likely to suffer identity theft. The growing prevalence of digital-advertising technology has led to greater adoption of ad blockers and information-protecting countermeasures, trends that could threaten the information-in-exchange-for-services relationship that exists between consumers and companies such as Google, Twitter, and Facebook. These trends may also threaten the content-in-exchange-for-advertising-impressions relationship publishers have with their digital readers.

It appears that one cost of the loss of privacy may be a loss of trust. If the actions of a few bad actors cause consumers to be more guarded with their personal data, the result may be fewer 'free' products and services, less access to digital content, and a lack of data for companies to use for business optimisation. The experience of Europe suggests that we might be better off using this data but using it wisely.

16. ACQUISITION PRICING

Acquiring a new customer with recurring revenue, such as a subscriber, is similar to other pricing questions in terms of the trade-off between volume and average rate. Where recurring-revenue acquisition pricing differs is in the potential to earn more profits from a customer in future periods. Profits from such a customer can increase, either because there are initial costs that are incurred upon acquisition (such as a sales commission) that do not occur in subsequent periods or because the revenue from the customer increases, such as when a customer moves from a promotional offer to a standard rate.

The likelihood of receiving operating margins from a new customer depends upon that individual's retention curve (the probability that he or she will be an active customer in future periods). As we have discussed in prior chapters, the analysis of retention curves is well suited to survival analysis, a field of econometrics pioneered by the healthcare industry. The higher the initial acquisition price, the longer a customer is expected to remain active. Survival analysis can estimate the incremental improvement in retention due to higher acquisition prices. Other econometric-modelling approaches, such as discrete-choice models, are well suited to analysing the effect of acquisition prices on a customer's probability of accepting the initial offer—in other words, his or her acquisition price elasticity. Both survival analysis and discrete choice models can be used to estimate a customer's renewal-price elasticity. In our experience, survival analysis is a superior tool for this analysis due to the nature of renewal decisions, where there can be many significant factors over many time periods in the renewal-pricing decision.

Customers acquired at lower prices tend to have a lower likelihood of remaining active, ceteris paribus, than customers acquired at higher prices. This phenomenon is due to acquisition offer price acting as a filter in the customer-acquisition process. Customers who accept service offers at a higher price are more confident in their purchase and less likely to 'try' the product to see if they like it. Customers who accept lower-priced offers tend to be closer to the margin of their preferences, which suggests they will be more likely than other customers to find that the product is not worth the nonpromotional price point.

Price elasticity for recurring-revenue customers tends to decline over time. In prior chapters, we have shown how targeted renewal-pricing strategies can use tenure (the length of time a customer has been active) as a guide to a customer's sensitivity to increases in renewal price. In acquisition pricing, it is helpful to design offers that mitigate churn risk for new customers so that they are more likely to accept their first renewal offer. One approach to mitigating churn risk is to provide a longer period of time under the promotional price.

One simplified acquisition-pricing strategy can be described as getting customers on as long a promotion term as possible for the lowest price possible. As is clearly evident from the description, this strategy has two contradictory objectives. In most cases, longer promotional terms require greater up-front payment amounts, while lower prices per period lower the initial payment. For example, a $10 per-month offer for one year is $120, and a $20 per-month offer for three months is $60. The $60 initial payment is appealing, but customers who receive a full-price renewal offer at the end of month three have a much lower likelihood of acceptance than a customer receiving a full-price renewal offer at the end of one year.

CASE STUDY

HOW ACQUISITION PRICING LED TO 152 PER CENT MORE REVENUE

OBJECTIVE: A large US publisher needed to improve campaign response rates without sacrificing revenue. They had direct mail response rates below 1 per cent for both lapsed and prospective subscribers, leading to a negative average ROI for the acquisition campaigns.

APPROACH: Mather Economics designed a test to compare subscription offers using a targeted customer-acquisition campaign. In the control group, customers were presented a single subscription offer for each product. In the target group, a range of offers were presented for each product, and subscribers were randomly presented offers within that range.

RESULTS: The test results showed significant improvement in acquisition of lapsed subscribers but mixed results amongst prospective subscribers. Response rates increased for lapsed and 'will-call' subscribers while staying largely the same for prospects. Revenue increased by 152 per cent for lapsed subscribers, which raised the ROI per order from –$4 to $34.

TARGETED ACQUISITION OFFERS RAISE REVENUE FOR LAPSED AND WILL CALL CUSTOMERS

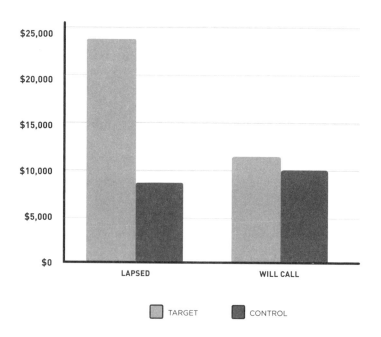

REMEMBER

- CLV is an excellent analytical framework for evaluating customer relationships and quantifying strategic options for customer-relationship management.

- Moving from 'one size fits fall' to more personalized customer interactions is a common thread across many applications of customer analytics, such as churn modelling, pricing strategies, and acquisition offers.

- Bottom-up forecasting is more accurate and effective than top-down or 'last year plus X per cent.'

- Holistic analysis of customer relationships include all revenue streams (such as advertising and audience revenue) so trade-offs between strategic options can be quantified.

- When analysing customer profitability, marginal costs are more important than average costs. Allocated overhead costs can bias customer-profitability analysis.

- The benefits of collecting more customer data likely outweigh the costs of additional data collection, which are often hard to observe.

- Subscriber-yield management, including targeted pricing, can increase revenue substantially while minimizing customer losses. This type of targeted pricing is a win-win for customers and companies, and companies have significant discretionary power in the degree to which prices are adjusted, including what data is included in the pricing calculations and the business rules that guide implementation.

SECTION 5.

CUSTOMER-EXPERIENCE TOOLS

This section describes customer-experience tools, which help to understand the needs of customers, employees, or anyone else. We use these for process improvements, product development, improved cooperation, and decision-making.

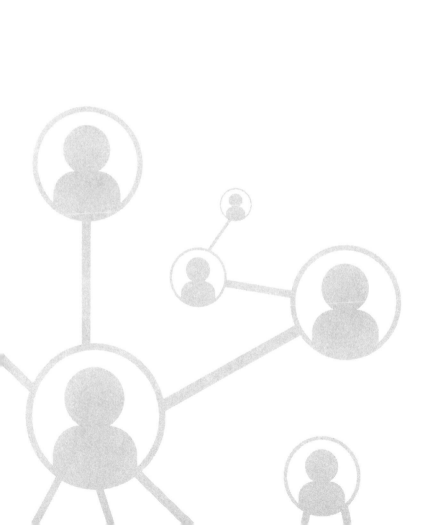

17. D.SCHOOL METHODOLOGY

A t NRC, we have regularly journeyed through the design-thinking experience, applying it afterwards in the real world when designing new brands, new websites, and a new magazine. We use the d.school methodology from Stanford University, invented by the Kelley brothers.[27] All material is provided free of charge at dschool.stanford. edu. Here is a brief summary how to conduct your own d.school.

DEFINE THE ASSIGNMENT

First, there has to be a clear assignment from an executive sponsor, who defines the main question of the design challenge. This assignment has to be defined as an experience that needs to be redesigned. For example, rather than asking how to redesign the sharing function on the website, it is better to ask how to redesign the sharing experi-

27 Tom and David Kelley, *Creative Confidence: Unleashing the Creative Potential Within Us All* (2013).

ence. This will bring stories to the surface about sharing, with all the emotions attached to that experience. It will make the group focused on needs instead of features.

COMPOSE THE GROUP

When the assignment is clear, the next step is organising a group of people. There must be at least two people, but there is no maximum number of participants. If everybody shares their thoughts with the entire group, it is better to not exceed ten participants because that will take too much time. Because activities during the d.school sessions are paired, there must be an even number of participants. In our experience, it is best to pick people from very different disciplines and backgrounds and to include actual customers in the d.school experience. The more extreme the user, the better the input because the goal is to explore new horizons, and a diverse group will broaden the resulting new ideas. There is no hierarchy in the group, although there is a facilitator who makes sure there is an Internet connection, a large screen, and a projector with sound.

ARRANGE FACILITIES

There may be arts-and-crafts supplies to build prototypes. Printed handouts from the d.school at dschool.stanford.edu are indispensable.

It helps to be all together in one very large room, both for group discussions and one-on-one interviews. If the room is not big enough for the latter, it is better to have extra accommodations for sessions between two people.

D.SCHOOL SESSION

At the d.school session itself, the group is divided in partner teams of two and goes through five phases: Empathise, Define, Ideate, Prototype, and Test. It should be possible to cover all the phases in one or two working days.

To start the first phase—empathising—participants begin a conversation by asking open-ended questions like, 'When was the last time you shared information with someone?' The partner digs deeper by asking 'Why?' often and asking what emotions were felt during the experience. It's important to treat the partner as an expert in the topic he or she is talking about and to try to experience what your partner experiences. Realise that the problems we try to solve are rarely our own; they are those of particular users. By bringing empathy into the conversation, we understand who the users are and what is important to them.

Next up is synthesising what has been said by the partner into insights and needs. These insights will lead to innovative solutions. Needs should be phrased as verbs. What is the user actually trying to achieve by sharing information? Try to write down the problem statement.

After nailing the needs, it is time to ideate. Create as many solutions as possible to address the user's problem. Then share the solutions with each other and listen to your partner's feedback. Fight the urge to defend your ideas. Grasp the opportunity to learn from your partner's emotions and motivations.

After reflecting on the first ideas, it is time to create one single, new solution and make a prototype for your partner. Make it as physical as possible so your partner can interact with it. The arts-and-crafts materials come in handy here. Now test it. Again, fight the urge to defend it. See how you partner misuses it, and learn from that.

At the end, get the group together and put the prototypes in the middle of the room. Who sees something they are curious to learn more about? Later, the group may present the best prototype to the executive sponsor. We guarantee you will present a human-centred service or product.

18. SERVICE DESIGN

T he service-design method can be very helpful to connect to customers and bring their needs and frustrations to the surface.

START WITH A BROAD QUESTION

The first step in service design is to define the actual question you have for your customers. When doing this for the first time, it is best to start with a broad, central question. This way the customers can lead you in any direction, which really is the right direction at that point. For example: 'What is the role of brand X in your life?' In a group brainstorm, you can deepen the questions you have for customers by letting different teams put post-its with their questions on the wall and present them to each other afterwards. This is the first phase of gaining empathy for customers. This usually results in several clusters of questions.

CREATE A DIARY

From these questions, make a diary for the respondents to fill out. This is done before the interviewing starts. We call this *sensitising*. This diary will get the respondents thinking about their customer experience, and creating it will make the interviewer step into the shoes of the customer even before the interview has taken place.

A diary allows respondents to be creative. They can draw or write or paste stickers. It may include topics like these:

- This is me . . .

- What I love doing . . .

- My working day . . .

- When I first used your product . . .

- That one great moment your product made me super happy . . .

- Here you disappointed me . . .

Respondents will complete the diaries in a couple of weeks and send them back to you. If you have any documentation on the customer, like product type, past complaints, turnover, or tenure, include that in your research and documentation. It is better to know the specific issues customers have already reported when you visit them in their house.

After receiving the diaries, the group comes together for a few hours and discusses every customer individually, writing down any new questions or insights you might want to use in the interview. Then it is time to go and ring the doorbell.

INTERVIEWING

The interviews should take place in the setting where customers use your product and where they feel comfortable. This makes a tremendous difference compared to interviewing at an anonymous place like your office or a research centre. These interviews typically take one to two hours.

Here is some practical advice for the interviews:

- Personally make an appointment with each respondent.

- Go in pairs, with one conducting the interview and the other capturing interview data.

- Talk about your own biases beforehand so you can ignore them during the interview and really listen.

- Have respondents sign a document indicating that they agree to be interviewed.

- Mention in the document that data is not distributed externally.

- Build some kind of rapport directly after arriving.

- The most effective attitude is open and inquisitive.

- Explicitly mention your goals for the interview.

- Fully charge your mobile and do not forget a charger.

- Capture the interview with an audio-recording app.

- Write down remarkable quotes.

- Annotate the minute of the quote to play it back.

- Write down the meaning of that quote for your organisation.

- Summarise: 'Did I understand correctly that you . . .?'

- Be silent—sometimes for an uncomfortable length of time—and respondents will talk more and deeper.

- Ask people to expand on feelings and emotions.

- Ask to take pictures of anything that strikes you in the house.

- Make a one-minute video with a remarkable quote.

CONDUCTING RESULTS

After the content of the interview has been well documented by writing down all the quotes and what they mean to you, it is time to get the group together and share insights. Make sure you book a room for at least three hours, with lots of brown paper on the wall and lots of post-its around. The different brown papers will form clusters of topics from the interviews. You can show each other the videos and bring customers to life. There are three things you can get from the interviews:

- a quick-fix list

- personae

- guiding principles

Guiding principles are things all respondents agree upon. These are actually part of your brand's DNA as perceived by customers.

The personae can be found by defining areas that differentiate your customers—areas of tension where there are significant differences in needs. Translate these areas to axes upon which you can plot your customers. Commonly you strive for two axes, resulting in four segments representing personae.

At NRC, we found differences in interest in interaction and the level of identification with the newspaper and the brand. Some subscribers want to interact with us and with each other, while others have no need to interact. Some feel part of the family or a group of special people; others just want qualitative journalism from an objective source.

19. ACTIVE LISTENING

The technique of active listening is described in Thomas Gordon's effective leadership training.[28] The goal of active—or empathic—listening is to get to understand a person's emotions and feelings. Through active listening, the listener lets the speaker know, *I understand your problem and how you feel about it, I am interested in what you are saying, and I am not judging you.* The listener unmistakably conveys this message through words and nonverbal behaviours like body language. In so doing, the listener encourages the speakers to fully express themselves free of interruption, criticism, or being told what to do.

The key thing is to say out loud what you think the other person really meant. It's looking for the deeper needs behind the words and trying to articulate these. It's like throwing darts. You will not hit the bullseye every time, but the attempt to understand the other person is always appreciated.

---

28   Thomas Gordon, *Leader Effectiveness Training* (1977).

Only when you know about each other's real needs can you start talking about possible solutions for a certain problem or situation. Needs are often not opposed; it's the solutions that meet opposition. It is possible to weigh the solutions by defining the extent to which the solution fits the different needs.

When you are practising active listening, it's important to

- be willing to let the other parties dominate the discussion;

- be attentive to what is being said;

- be careful not to interrupt;

- use open-ended questions;

- be sensitive to the emotions being expressed; and

- reflect back to the other party and the feelings behind what is said.

Some people can have a hard time listening actively. Guessing what another person means can feel like you are admitting the other person is right and you are not. But that is not what it is about. Active listening is about checking whether you understood the other correctly. It is an act of empathy that makes the other feel heard.

20. NEEDS MATRIX

The complexity of business issues can be overwhelming. Everyone, from customers to top management, has needs to balance. Different departments have different interests; individuals within departments have different goals. Finance wants budget discipline, IT wants reliability, stockholders want return on investment, and employees want to feel good about what they are doing. There may be ethical questions, there are often legal aspects, and last but not least, there may be suppliers involved from outside the company.

When designing solutions for all these needs, we developed a matrix that leans on the Gordon method of active listening. This means we try to figure out the deeper need of the other person without judging—just checking whether we understood things correctly.

Let us look at a practical example of how we use this matrix. The case is as follows. After being successful for many years selling news subscriptions with an iPad, NRC had several problems. We felt that a growing number of people were buying the iPad for the sake of the iPad. There was legislation coming up that would force us to present the iPad as a loan, thus becoming a bank, with all the strict legal implications that entails. The number of new subscribers was down, but the amount of work was the same. We felt that delivery time was too long to meet current standards and that the process had become too complicated over the course of time. Also, the number of customers not paying correctly went up sharply after years with very few problems. There was no simple solution for all of these issues. The number of departments and stakeholders involved was huge and included external suppliers.

At first, the problem solver Mira Pasveer talked to the NRC stakeholders one by one and asked what their needs were when it came to the iPad offering. She identified over twenty different needs that were placed in the rows of the matrix. In the same interviews, the problem solver asked what hypothetical solutions the stakeholders had. It is important to be as creative as possible with solutions. We want volume here. The problem solver must motivate the stakeholder to suggest as many solutions as possible, even crazy ones. These solutions were placed in the columns.

When it comes to active listening, it is important that everyone have an equal opportunity to be heard and seen. Therefore, in the needs-matrix methodology, all stakeholders must gather in one room and block one hour (preferably two) in their agendas. It is better to postpone the meeting than to have a particular stakeholder be unable to attend the meeting physically.

In this meeting, Mira first went through the needs, row by row. Did she understand the need correctly? Did the group understand the definition of the need? Were there any needs missing? Talking about a subject in a group usually brings up previously hidden feelings. We prefer to have the matrix on a computer connected to a large screen so that we can add or alter needs live, actively showing the stakeholder we are listening. Then, solutions are discussed in a similar fashion.

Now that everybody in the group feels listened to, it is time to weigh the solutions. We prefer to work horizontally, discussing the solutions one by one with regard to a specific need. We use a five-point scale ranging from double minus (not helping at all) to double plus (great solution for that need).

The whole group has to—and usually will—agree on one answer per cell. After this exercise, a picture will arise of which solution is addressing the most needs. Usually, we end up deciding which need weighs most heavily, and then reach an agreement on the right solution. Sometimes a combination of solutions is found to address most needs.

With very complex issues, the needs matrix is a solution to making business decisions while actively listening to everybody. The group ends up implementing these solutions with far more motivation—and the ideas are typically much better—than in the classical division of brains (management) figuring out a solution and hands (employees) executing it.

NEEDS / SOLUTIONS	100 Euro Initial Payment	Borrow max 250 Euro	2/4 options	Continue	Stop doing	Lease agreement	Credit agreement
Acquisition of at least 3,000 per year	-1	-2	-1	1	-2	-1	-1
Less switching to iPad	1	2	0	-1	2	1	1
Simple fullfillment	0	0	0	0	2	-2	-2
Smaller difference between offers in contract and list price	-1	-2	1	1	2	1	1
Simplicity in our offers (overview for customers)	0	0	1	0	1	-1	-2
Fewer defaulters	1	2	-1	-1	1	-1	1
Not becoming a bank	0	1	0	0	1	0	-2
Sell core product (news not devices)	-1	-1	-1	-1	2	-1	-1
Customers who want to use NRC	0	0	-1	-1	1	-1	-1
Comply with law	-1	1	-1	-1	1	1	1
No fine	-1	1		-1	1	1	1
No bad PR	-1	1	-1	-1	1	1	1
Less work for several departments	-1	-1	-1	-1	2	-2	-2
Current subscribers have a good feeling about our marketing efforts	-1	-1	-1	-1	1	-1	-1
Wait for iPhone7	1	1	1	1	-1	1	1
Wait and see what the bank and telecom business will do	1	1	1	1	-1	-1	-1
Scores	-5	2	-6	-6	15	-6	-7

Needs matrix iPad offerings.

REMEMBER

- The d.school method ensures your process or product is based on real needs.

- Ask broad questions in service design so customers lead you in the right direction.

- Become an active listener by reflecting the feelings behind what has been said.

- Make a needs matrix when complexity is high or many stakeholders are involved.

CONCLUSION

Our objective in writing this book was to share the insights we have learned from combining the fields of customer experience and customer analytics. We have seen that the combination of rigorous customer-relationship building and quantitative analysis of those relationships is a winning strategy in this era of recurring-revenue business models and ever-present customer data.

Taken separately, the fields of customer experience and customer analytics have much to offer, and they are in high demand in their own rights. Through our collaboration, we have realised that when combined, these fields are more than the sum of their parts, and we have seen that using the insights and the tools described in sections 4 and 5 of this book can help companies succeed in the evolving economy we live in, which we have dubbed the Relationship Economy. Customer experience, when quantified, makes a soft subject manageable and rigorous. Customer analytics, when applied through the process of optimising customer relationships, becomes revenue generating and approachable.

Our treatment of these subjects was designed to avoid the esoteric and arcane details of each discipline in favour of real-world examples and case studies described with a minimum of jargon. We also hoped to punch through the hype around big data to focus on what data analysis can do for companies—in the right operational context and within the strategic framework of customer-experience management—to generate a return on the investment.

We wanted to share best practices in using KPIs to support culture as well as performance, in combining business people and data teams, and in listening to customers, both through what they say and through data. We hope this encourages you to test new pricing strategies by using target and control groups and to optimise customer acquisition through the use of intelligent thresholds.

The key concepts in this book regarding the use of data are to make sure there is a business case before undertaking a big-data project, to remember there are costs in terms of customer trust and privacy from collecting data, and to combine analytics with management vision and initiative to achieve performance gains.

In the field of customer experience, we focused on how to acquire the right customers and keep the relationship going in the long term. We also discussed methodologies to connect to customers by using empathy and better understand their needs.

Our work is not over with this book. We continue to evolve together with our partners. We invite you to join the community of people with a deep understanding of the Relationship Economy.

We are curious to learn from your challenges and success stories. You can reach us at matt@mathereconomics.com, xavier@mathereconomics.com, and matthijs@mathereconomics.com. We promise we will answer every e-mail.

Safe travels.

ABOUT THE AUTHORS

MATT LINDSAY is president of the Atlanta-based Mather Economics, one of the fastest-growing private companies in the United States. Matt has over twenty years of experience helping businesses improve performance through pricing strategies and predictive models for clients including the Intercontinental Exchange, Gannett, The Home Depot, NRG Energy, IHG, McClatchy, the Everglades Foundation, Dow Jones, and *The New York Times*. Matt began his consulting career with Arthur Andersen and has also worked with the Corporate Economics Group. Matt is a sought-after expert and frequently speaks at media industry events including the News Media Alliance's MediaXchange, the INMA World Congress, and the WAN-IFRA World Newspaper Conference. Matt holds a doctorate in economics from the University of Georgia, a master's in applied economics from Clemson University, and an undergraduate degree in economics from the University of Georgia.

MATTHIJS VAN DE PEPPEL has been working in the newspaper industry for over ten years. Starting his career as a circulation marketer, he quickly developed as an online shop manager, online marketer, and project manager. Now as the manager of the data-intelligence and customer-relationship management team at NRC Media, a quality Dutch news organisation, Matthijs is responsible for bringing data insights into decision making and amplifying the voice of the customer. Matthijs holds a bachelor's degree in Dutch language and culture and a master's in organisational science from the University of Utrecht, and he attends a postgraduate curriculum for business analytics and data science at the Vrije Universiteit Amsterdam.

XAVIER VAN LEEUWE has over ten years of experience as a marketing executive at NRC, Telegraaf Media Groep, and de Persgroep. At the Amsterdam-based news organisation NRC, Xavier lead the transformation of his team by building a customer-centric and data-rich culture at a news organisation with 189 years of heritage. Prior to being a media executive, he worked for several years as a financial and political journalist in the Netherlands. Xavier started his career as a researcher for the United Nations in Geneva. He has been a speaker at several conferences in Europe, the United States, and South America. Xavier is an active marketing tech blogger for INMA.org and publishes a weekly free newsletter you can subscribe to at *Changemediaforgood.com*. Xavier holds a cum laude master's in business administration and a degree in journalism from Erasmus University Rotterdam.

NRC MEDIA is a Dutch news organisation that was founded in 1828. There are 7.5 million households in the Netherlands and 2.4 million newspaper copies distributed daily. NRC has over 265,000 active subscribers. Its news website, NRC.nl, generates over twenty million monthly page views. The company has 360 employees, and its revenue ratio is 81 per cent subscriber income and 19 per cent advertising.

MATHER ECONOMICS is a global consulting firm that applies a combination of proprietary analytical tools and operational expertise to help businesses better understand customers and, in turn, develop and implement pricing strategies that maximise operating margins, grow revenue, and improve customer loyalty. Mather was founded in 2002 and has forty employees. Mather assists about five hundred clients with their recurring-revenue yield management. These clients in turn serve thirty million households, with Mather analysing over $4 billion a year in revenue generated by these households.

Mather Economics
+1 770 993 4111
1215 Hightower Trail, A-100
Atlanta, GA 30350
United States

ACKNOWLEDGMENTS

This book would not have been possible without the immense help of our beloved and respected colleagues at NRC and Mediahuis. First and foremost we thank Heiko Imelman, who set us on the right course by keeping the data warehouse simple. Heiko also introduced us to the power of empathy. We also thank Gert Ysebaert, Caspar van Rhijn, Rien van Beemen, Wilbert Schutrups, Peter Vandermeersch, Mira Pasveer, Eefje Pater, Lucas Vos, Saoendy Pahladsingh, Marloes Berger, Dennis Lotten, Linda Reinders, Arthur Passtoors, Stephan Maat, Niels Hoedjes, Iris Bosma, Sebastiaan Verhaar, Martijn Zanen, Femke van Welsenes, Joleen van der Zwan, Marnix van Buuren, Niels Vlug, Adriaan Rekker, Mirjam Kruisman, Lia Jonas, and Omid Holterman.

We are grateful to our colleagues at Mather Economics: Arvid Tchivzhel, Dustin Tetley, Matthew Lulay, Adrian Stavaru, Jack Curran, Andrew Carstensen, Alicia Queen, Brandon Williams, Tom Slusher, Patrick Smith, Steve Padgett, Bob Terzotis, Shawn DeWeese, Brian Brown, Marigrace Davis, Briana Garcia, Chuck Currin, Judy Drobinski, and all of the seniors and analysts on the team.

We thank our proofreaders: WAN-IFRA's Vincent Peyregne and Dean Roper; Ken Doctor of Newsonomics; customer-experience gurus Willem Aanen and Sydney Brouwer; Tim Corbett, and Earl Wilkinson at INMA; Marit Coehoorn and Erik Roscam Abbing at Livework; Nick Poldermans at Rabobank; Yourzine's Jimmy de Vreede for his in-depth comments; and our publisher, Advantage, with Eland Mann, Kirby Andersen, Helen Harris, Peter Berry, and Katie Biondo. Also many thanks to Jan Dirk van Abshoven for introducing us to the world of active listening. We would also like to thank Hans Nijenhuis, who introduced us—Matt, Matthijs, and Xavier—to each other four years ago.

We thank our families and wives, Annie, Arieke, and Wietske, who supported us in writing this book.

SOURCES

Ariely, Dan. *Predictably Irrational: The Hidden Forces That Shape Our Decisions.* New York: HarperCollins, 2009.

Baxter, Robbie K. *The Membership Economy: Find Your Superusers, Master the Forever Transaction, and Build Recurring Revenue.* McGraw-Hill Education, 2015.

Collins, Jim. *Good to Great: Why Some Companies Make the Leap . . . And Others Don't.* New York: HarperCollins, 2001.

Davenport, Thomas H. "Analytics 3.0." *Harvard Business Review,* December 2013.

Davenport, Thomas H. et al., "Data to Knowledge to Results: Building an Analytical Capability." *California Management Review* 43, no. 2 (2001).

Duhigg, Charles. *The Power of Habit: Why We Do What We Do in Life and Business.* New York: Random House, 2012.

Forrester. "Global Heat Map." 2015. Accessed October 20, 2016. http://heatmap.forrestertools.com/.

Gordon, Thomas. *Leader Effectiveness Training: L.E.T.* New York: The Berkley Publishing Group, 1977.

Kelley, David and Tom Kelley. *Creative Confidence: Unleashing the Creative Potential Within Us All.* New York: Crown Business, 2013.

Laney, Doug. "3D Data Management: Controlling Data Volume, Velocity and Variety." *META Group*, February 2001.

Poundstone, William. *Priceless: The Myth of Fair Value (and How to Take Advantage of It).* New York: Hill and Wang, 2011.

Putnam, Robert D. *Bowling Alone: The Collapse and Revival of American Community.* Simon & Schuster Paperbacks, 2001.

Thaler, Richard. "Mental accounting and consumer choice." *Marketing Science* 4 (1985): 199–214.

Wang, Ting, Lih-Bin Oh, Kanliang Wang, and Yufei Yuan. "User adoption and purchasing intention after free trial: an empirical study of mobile newspapers." *Information Systems and e-Business Management* 11 (2012).

WAN-IFRA. *World Press Trends Report. 2016.*

Zuora. *The Subscription Economy Index.* 2016.

INDEX

A

A/B testing, 59
account tenure, 128
acquisition
   channel, 107, 126–127
   customers and, 116
   pricing, 75, 107, 139–142
   threshold, 66–67
active listening, 91, 157–158, 159–161
advertising
   demographics and, 31, 123
   dissatisfaction with, 136–137
   revenue from, 21, 119–120, 128, 130, 131
   targeted, 31, 136
analytics. *See* data
anchoring, 67
audit bureau, 18–19, 25, 63, 98

B

big data. *See also* data
   definition of, 30
   misconceptions of, 36
   value of, 31–32, 34–36, 166

C

centralised data team, 13–14

D

data
  demographics and, 123, 134
  failure of, 14, 35–36
  individual sales, 73
  retention, 33, 126
  storage, 34
  trial subscriptions and, 68
  use of, 31–32, 136
  value of, 12–13, 15
data collection
  case study of, 33, 39–40
  ethics of, 38
  Listener and, 119–120
  purpose of, 3, 34
data mining, 31–32
decentralised data teams, 15
discrete choice models, 39, 104, 140
d.school, 97, 147–150

E

employees
  customer empathy by, 87, 91
  KPIs for, 76
  performance of, 72–73, 75
  value of, 72

F

Facebook, 31
Ford, Henry, 90–91
forecasting, 43, 115–117

R

S

T

Y

yield management, 51, 128–129, 134